Religious Education: Philosophical Perspectives

Introductory Studies in Philosophy of Education

Series Editors: PHILIP SNELDERS and COLIN WRINGE

Religious Education: Philosophical Perspectives

JOHN SEALEY

London
GEORGE ALLEN & UNWIN
Boston   Sydney

George Allen & Unwin (Publishers) Ltd,
40 Museum Street, London WC1A 1LU, UK

George Allen & Unwin (Publishers) Ltd,
Park Lane, Hemel Hempstead, Herts HP2 4TE, UK

Allen & Unwin, Inc.,
Fifty Cross Street, Winchester, Mass. 01890, USA

George Allen & Unwin Australia Pty Ltd,
8 Napier Street, North Sydney, NSW 2060, Australia

First published in 1985

British Library Cataloguing in Publication Data

Sealey, John
    Religious education.—(Introductory studies in
philosophy of education)
1. Religious education—Teaching methods
I. Title   II. Series
200'.7'1   BV1475.2
ISBN 0-04-370130-2
ISBN 0-04-370131-0 Pbk

Library of Congress Cataloging in Publication Data

Sealey, John.
    Religious education.
(Introductory studies in philosophy of education)
Bibliography: p.
Includes index.
1. Religious education—Philosophy. I. Title.
II. Series.
BL42.S42 1984   200'.7   84-12287
ISBN 0-04-370130-2 (alk. paper)
ISBN 0-04-370131-0 (pbk. : alk. paper)

Set in 10 on 11 point Plantin by Grove Graphics, Tring, Hertfordshire
and printed in Great Britain
by
Biddles Ltd, Guildford, Surrey

Contents

Editors' Foreword

Books that are available to students of philosophy of education may, in general, be divided into two types. There are collections of essays and articles making up a more or less random selection; and there are books which explore a single theme or argument in depth but, having been written to break new ground, are often unsuitable for general readers or those near the beginning of their course. The Introductory Studies in Philosophy of Education are intended to fill what is widely regarded as an important gap in this range.

The series aims to provide a collection of short, readable works which, besides being philosophically sound, will seem relevant and accessible to future and existing teachers without a previous knowledge of philosophy or of philosophy of education. In the planning of the series account has necessarily been taken of the tendency of present-day courses of teacher education to follow a more integrated and less discipline-based pattern than formerly. Account has also been taken of the fact that students on three- and four-year courses, as well as those on shorter postgraduate and in-service courses, quite understandably expect their theoretical studies to have a clear bearing on their practical concerns, and on their dealings with children. Each book, therefore, starts from a real and widely recognized problem in the educational field, and explores the main philosophical approaches which illuminate and clarify it, or suggests a coherent standpoint even when it does not claim to provide a solution. Attention is paid to the work of both mainstream philosophers and philosophers of education. For students who wish to pursue particular questions in depth, each book contains a bibliographical essay or a substantial list of suggestions for further reading. It is intended that a full range of the main topics recently discussed by philosophers of education should eventually be covered by the series.

Besides having considerable experience in the teaching of philosophy of education, the majority of authors writing in the series have already received some recognition in their particular fields. In addition, therefore, to reviewing and criticizing existing work, each author has his or her own positive contribution to make to further discussion.

The majority of books on religious education are written by those who are themselves adherents of particular religious beliefs and such books almost invariably reflect their authors' religious inclinations. Given the characteristically proselytizing quality of many religions, especially Christianity and Islam, this is hardly surprising. Such religions require commitment of their followers, rather than neutrality. However understandable this state of affairs may be, it is also a reason for disquiet, particularly among the secular majority. A critical look at certain key aspects in religious education from a secular point of view is long overdue.

John Sealey provides such an appraisal, and offers a critical survey of frequently debated questions in religious education. How can one speak of 'knowledge' as opposed to 'belief' in religion? What sort of theory lies behind religious education and how does it make sense? Does indoctrination play a part in RE? His conclusions will be welcomed by many but felt to be controversial by others: namely, that religion as a school subject can be as 'secular' as history or literature without being superficial; and that 'religiousness' or 'being religious' or even the holding of a 'life stance' on the part of a teacher or pupil is no longer essential in the teaching and learning of religion as an educational subject.

John Sealey has taught in a variety of schools and universities and has previously published several articles on the philosophy of education and religion. He is also the author of educational textbooks in history, poetry and music, and brings considerable experience to bear on this least tractable of subjects on the school timetable.

PHILIP SNELDERS
COLIN WRINGE

Preface

Renford Bambrough once remarked 'There is no shallow end in philosophy'. This book is an introduction to the philosophy of religious education in the sense that while it raises important philosophical issues in RE it does not purport to follow any argument to a conclusion or to incorporate all the features that a theory or idea may comprise. *Religious Education: Philosophical Perspectives* is to be seen as an example of philosophy of RE at work, imperfect though this may be, and not merely as a description of that activity. In this sense the reader is taken almost immediately into a maelstrom where he may observe at first hand the cut and thrust of the philosopher's challenges that go to make up the activity of philosophy. There is no shallow end in the philosophy of RE either.

I wish to express my warmest thanks to Philip Snelders, not simply for giving me the opportunity to write this book in the series that was his brainchild, and for his thoughtful advice during its writing, but more especially for his kindness and help to me over a period of many years and through the difficulties those years have sometimes brought.

I have been helped in the writing of this book by many people in the field of RE. Some, including most of those whose work I have criticized in the following pages, have been of particular help in personal correspondence with me. I am glad to be able to acknowledge my debt to them. To my wife Marion I offer my thanks for her patience and support in my work — as ever.

I am grateful to the editors and publishers of the following journals for allowing me to reproduce in Chapter 4 material already published: to the *British Journal of Religious Education*, vol. 5, no. 1, 1982, for parts of 'Another look at Smart's six-dimensional account of religion'; and to the *Journal of Philosophy of Education*, vol. 17, no. 2, 1983, for 'Religious education: a component of moral education?'.

John A. Sealey

Pray, what is religious education?
(Alfred North Whitehead)

1

A Philosophical Approach to Problems in Religious Education

An inspector visiting a school in the midlands in 1888 reported to the governing church authorities that the children ought to have 'more varied occupations' than the usual bible readings, writing and counting. When the vicar read the inspector's report he said: 'Anything which teaches the tinys to use their funny little fingers must be useful to them, though I can't help thinking that knitting and sewing and writing on a slate is good enough' (Sealey, 1970, pp. 16–17). The vicar seems not to have studied philosophy of education. Had he seriously asked himself whether it was indeed appropriate for the school to teach anything that was useful? There were many things that could be 'usefully' learnt by the fingers of the poor in 1888 but I doubt if the vicar would have approved them all. Did the vicar have his reasons for thinking that 'knitting and sewing and writing on a slate' were 'good enough'? And if he did, what were they 'good enough' for?

Whatever we think of this vicar's views, and the assumptions and prejudices that may have underlain them, we cannot escape the issue that there is no difference in kind between the vicar and teachers of today if we, too, do not ask ourselves relevant questions and supply rational answers concerning educational situations. The subject matter in a school curriculum, like the date, may have changed; attitudes do not always change so easily. In questioning what we think we know, what we think ought to be taught; in asking what objectives there might reasonably be for education, and so on, we have already begun to philosophize.

'Philosophy' is sometimes a frightening word. It need not be so. Put it this way: we tend to feel 'safe' with a curriculum subject once we know the facts and have a fair degree of competence within the area. In religion, for instance, an RE teacher schooled in a Christian tradition will have no bother in putting together material for a lesson on the parables of Jesus or the idea of Christian baptism. A Muslim will be quite at home in preparing lessons on the life of Mohammed or the early expansion of Islam. For most of the major religious groups represented in Britain today – Christian, Muslim, Jewish, Sikh, Hindu – there exist hundreds of books and much published material to help the RE teacher plan the available information for his lessons, systematize his themes and organize his teaching techniques. Similarly there is a wide literature on the psychological, sociological and historical aspects of teaching religion to children. It might seem on the face of it that all this readily available material poses for the RE teacher only the problem of choice. What items of information or what topical issues shall I use for this particular theme and how shall I proceed?

Unfortunately for this apparently idyllic state of affairs, there are problems in RE that find no clear answer in textbooks, official syllabuses and teaching guides. There are problems that cannot be resolved by the production of new information or procedures for teaching. They are problems that arise *from* the facts; problems of meaning and of justification. It is this area that constitutes the philosophy of RE. For example, what do we *mean* when we speak of religious 'knowledge'? Does it *matter* what is taught in RE? What sort of thing would I be doing if I were indoctrinating? If we are to take RE seriously then the uncertainty produced by these philosophical questions has to be faced. And to face them squarely requires a shift in our approach; not a more difficult approach, but a different one. The first startling thing about philosophy, it might be discovered, is that there are usually no final answers. An unnerving experience, perhaps, but the joy in that particular realization is a significant step forward in our knowledge: for at least we shall *know* that we don't know.

I shall attempt, first, to direct attention to some of those areas in RE that *seem* to be 'safe'. That is to say, I shall question some things that often go unquestioned because they appear to have plenty of backing in fact and opinion. Secondly, I shall attempt to open fresh avenues of inquiry into areas already disputed. It is one thing to be confused or made undecided as to how we are to proceed in RE by the proliferation of published classroom texts, by syllabuses and by teaching aids. It is quite another, and more disturbing, matter to find ourselves in the dark about the grounds, the reasons, for our decisions. For example, given a choice of teaching material for fourth form RE studies between, say, that concerned with encouraging 'pupils to identify with problems of human need and deprivation' (Dudley, 1979, p. 39) and material concerned with getting pupils to 'understand the meaning of particular religious beliefs' (Hampshire, 1978, p. 27), are we sure of our grounds in thinking that both schemes of study are in fact *religious* studies, as opposed to, say, economics, politics, ethics, or sociology? In a word, can we honestly say we know what does and what does not constitute an area of study in RE? To get clear on this issue is to raise philosophical questions directly related to RE. This is why, in more general terms, we may doubt that the vicar in the midlands school had studied philosophy of education, for we may question his understanding of the educational enterprise, his competence to judge what was 'good enough' for children, and so on.

Philosophical problems in RE, then, arise as a result of what is claimed for the subject and from the nature of religion itself. The philosophy of RE is not another 'scheme' for teaching religion and offers no new information on the subject. It plays the less ebullient but none the less important role of providing the classroom teacher with the tools whereby he may himself constructively criticize what is commonly talked about in RE. In so doing, the teacher is bound to reappraise, perhaps refine and even redefine, the nature of his task in the classroom.

We want to know what sort of grounds there might be for deciding whether what we call 'religion' has any rational basis in our understanding of the world. Can we make a claim to religious *knowledge*? Or must we settle for what some people would say is something less, mere 'belief' or an emotional dependence on mythical forces – experiences we may hesitate to include in a highly sophisticated process of public education? Or perhaps we must make do with, at most, a descriptive account of religion involving not an exploration of religious knowledge but only a historical, sociological, or psychological examination of what others experience, effectively avoiding the problem of religious knowledge. One of the major problems of religious knowledge comes from the 'positivist' theistic challenge: 'What would count *against* belief in God?' According to Antony Flew, if a statement is not falsifiable, that is, if it cannot be disproved in principle, then it cannot be a statement at all; it can be proved neither true nor false and is therefore nonsense. All assertions about God, so runs the argument, are compatible. Even the notorious problem of evil is explained away by religious believers. Eventually, says Flew, attempts to prove the existence of God fail in 'the death by a thousand qualifications' (Flew and MacIntyre, 1955, ch. VI, s. A, p. 97).

If it can be maintained that religion cannot be said to be 'true', like science, history, or mathematics, how can it be justified as an aspect of the 'real' external world which schools prepare children for? If we are merely to regard religious scriptures as 'literature', and if we are able to describe devotional attitudes to deity only in terms of a need to satisfy some purely subjective, psychologically based longing, how can we speak of *religious* knowledge? Surely, it may be argued, if religion can claim to be a fit subject for education, in view of these difficulties, so can magic, astrology and superstition of all kinds. Why should we burden an overloaded school timetable with matters that appear to be unknowable? What rational lines of thought can help us decide what to teach as 'religion'? Lines of demarcation, as well as claims to knowledge, are not just useful as a guide for what the RE teacher is to teach. They are necessary to his being sure, or to his having good grounds for the claim, that what he is teaching *is* religion and not, say, politics, history, or literature.

If RE can be justified as a curriculum subject on rational grounds, similar to those we might offer for teaching other subjects, what would a 'religiously educated' person look like? What skills, qualities, attitudes, and so on, would he have to exhibit? We may take it as agreed, at least in principle, that any form of 'confessional' teaching of religion would be out of place in public education. But could we say that a practising Muslim, for example, who had never had formal instruction in his religion was not in some way 'religiously educated'? While it would seem unreasonable, on the face of it, to deny that some sort of education must have taken place, it would also seem unreasonable to regard such a person as 'educated' in a more general sense. For the impression given is that such a person is so educated *in virtue of* his knowledge of doctrines, his religious attitudes and behaviour and his commitment to one distinctive set of beliefs to the exclusion of others. And at this point we may find ourselves wondering, is this truly what I would describe as an 'educated' person in *any* sense? How would we react to the phrase 'atheistically educated' or 'criminally educated'?

Let us consider that a coherent response lies in the direction of the question 'What is an *educated* person?'. In asking this we may begin to see that an examination of the notion of a *religiously* educated person may be fruitless in the sense that we could not recognize as 'education' the limitations imposed by such a narrow band of skills and knowledge. For although we cannot say of a committed Muslim that he is not educated in some narrowly defined sense, we shall want to say that this is not what is to be understood by the notion of 'the educated person'.

Does this mean that the idea of a 'religiously educated' person is misconceived, and that what we really mean be a 'religiously educated' person is someone whose education has included a study of religion? Perhaps there is no need to go into any depth of debate on the issue. 'I frankly have no idea what it means to be a "religiously educated person"', says Alan Harris (1970, p. 97). We might say something similar of 'religious education'. We might say, what is 'religious education' if not education with a religious component? And if we have now reduced the problem to asking for the characteristics of the 'educated person', then the question for us in this philosophical appraisal of RE is, is what is taught in RE adequate in terms of educational form and content?

Considering 'religious education', then, as distinct from the 'religiously educated' person, we might ask, what are some of the theories underlying the teaching of religion today? In what ways do theorists use religious material? Are there outstanding problems in current approaches? The shift from a 'confessional' approach is evident in the literature but that does not mean there is anything like agreement on the educational underpinning of RE. We shall look briefly at three different theories. Certain theories, certain attitudes in RE are, not surprisingly, more influential than others. The notion of 'implicit' religion is one area we can usefully examine. Does it make sense to distinguish between 'implicit' and 'explicit' religion? Ninian Smart (Smart and Horder, 1975, ch. 1) has made much of the distinction and the RE teacher will want to know something of the logic that lies behind it. Some explanation is to be found in Smart's justification for his well-known six-dimensional account of religion. But, we might ask, how can it be claimed that, for instance, communism is a manifestation of religion? Or again, how would we know that 'ritual' is a form of *religion*?

Some theorists see religion as a form of ethical knowledge. According to John Wilson (in Wilson, 1971, for example), since religion has its origin in the emotions and emotions are closely connected to moral knowledge, religion is to be taught as part of moral education. However we look at it, the teacher will want to ask not merely whether there is a relationship between the emotions and religion (which there obviously is) but whether central characteristics in religion (worship, for example) can be dependent upon emotional features for their distinctiveness as *religion*. After all, certain propositional elements in religion (for example, that God exists) can hardly depend on how we *feel* about it.

Raymond Holley (1978) has argued that there is an important distinction to be made between 'religious understanding' and 'scholarly understanding', and one is led to think that while 'scholarly understanding' is alone satisfactory for other subjects, RE requires the additional intellectual dimensions of 'religious understanding'. What substance is there in this distinction? Is it the case that teachers of RE have for so long neglected the 'ontic' values discerned through 'religious understanding'?

Turning from the theories for the moment, what of the *function* religion is thought to have in RE? Some Agreed Syllabuses and writers speak of pupils' being encouraged to find the 'truth' and to make a 'choice' in religion. Is there a special sense of 'truth' here? The implication is that there is, and one suspects that it is the 'truth' of the committed religious believer. If this is so, the agnostic or humanist, together with the inquiring teacher, will wish to press the question 'What significance can this special kind of "truth" and "choice" have for a liberal education in which there is no presumption in favour of commitment to religion?'.

The teacher will want to ask why these changes in content and emphasis have come about in view of the professed non-confessional attitude in contemporary RE. One reply that might be given is that Britain is now a multi-cultural, multi-racial and multi-religious society. Changes in the syllabuses reflect changes in society. When Britain was a Christian society what need was there to teach Sikhism or humanism? Is it not appropriate in view of the many different religious or religious-type belief systems now widespread in Britain that children should be given the knowledge and skills needed to make their own choice in the search for truth? Further, it might be argued, do children not need to know how to handle problems concerning drug-taking, the effects of TV, and so on, in the modern world? And surely the pupil will need to know the difference between 'right' and 'wrong'? And is it not true today that the educated person needs to know about the effects of world over-population, about conserving the environment, about problems facing trade unions and management and other global problems?

Then there is the more academic side of the coin. It is assumed by some that in the interests of developing the rational mind pupils should be given the academic knowledge and intellectual skills to decide for themselves what sort of choice, within or outside religion, they may make. Is it educationally appropriate to urge pupils to go beyond the acquisition of knowledge and critical skill and to make commitments? Would we teach politics in the same way and expect pupils, *qua* pupils, to opt for either the Monday Club or the Young Communist League? (Or would these two alternatives be religious choices in Smart's 'implicit' sense?) In what educational sense is the study of religion also a search for the student's own personality, as some would assert?

It may be questioned whether RE should be enlarged to the extent that some syllabuses appear to favour, despite the proffered justification. Has the question about what 'religion' is, about what its boundaries might be, been given the serious consideration it deserves? Can we indeed justify the teaching of communism, fascism and humanism in RE? And is it not possible that the idea of 'religious morality' is a contradiction in terms? – for we may well confront serious arguments to support the view that religious behavioural patterns have no necessary connection with the secular morality by which many people live.

Given the openness of the intellectual climate in which schools now operate, is it not arguable that RE is no more than a hangover from the time when Britain was Christian, and that now RE is at best obsolete and at worst a form of indoctrination? Moreover, is indoctrination not inevitable in RE in view of the fact that religion in its Western forms is essentially a proselytizing movement calling for commitment? And is not the danger of the 'faith commitment' – possibly an anti-educational experience – especially great where RE is taught by teachers who are themselves committed? On the other hand, if it is not disputed that there is such a thing

6

as religious experience in the world should not pupils be so taught that they will be able to make their own commitment to religion at some stage?

Changes in subject material within RE now include a study of religions other than Christianity. That is one change of attitude, and clearly a natural development in an RE that is no longer bound to a single, Christian, religious tradition. Other attitudes have developed, however, which a secular society might wish to question. There is an increased involvement in moral education within RE, coupled with a discernible desire to regard RE as a sort of spinal cord in the corpus of the curriculum. Then there is the further aspect, projected by many Agreed Syllabuses and writers in the field, that RE must be utilitarian in character either as a guide to how pupils should behave or as a means by which they can discover their own identity. The question such attitudes raise is whether there is any justification for viewing one area of education among many as a super-subject able alone to direct life and its meaning. Such views also highlight a significant aspect of the nature of education as a whole, for they raise the question of whether a process of education is primarily concerned with the *practice* (what I shall call 'first order' activities) of the various forms of human experience; or, on the other hand, whether education can be conceived as essentially a *study* of human experience (a 'second order' process) intended to bring young people to the *threshold* of first order experience. And if the latter view is held, then what possible educational reason could there be for the act of worship in schools, since such an activity can hardly be considered as 'study'?

In order to avoid difficulties that attach to the idea of personal engagement in religion, it has been proposed that RE ought to be interpreted as teaching 'about' religion. Yet it could be argued that the vagueness of the phrase contributes nothing to the debate on whether and in what sense 'engagement' is to be avoided.

Summary of Chapter 1

A philosophical approach to RE is different in character from other studies that may be used to help form educational theory. Philosophy thrives not on settling disputes or proposing theories but on an unending search for weaknesses or fallacies within existing theories. Every attempted refutation of a theory, as Karl Popper might say, especially of a good theory, is a step towards progress. Questions of the sort raised in this chapter are intended to facilitate, indeed to provoke, progress in RE.

2

Religion and Knowledge

If we wish to be clear about what to teach in RE then we need to know, as far as possible, what criteria there are for deciding that some things can legitimately be taught *as* religion and others not. That is, there must be certain grounds for being able to distinguish between, say, history and religion. Criteria for deciding what something is act like rules in a game. Without rules we should not know that a certain complex of activities constituted a game, let alone what that game might be. Consider the statement 'Islam/power/money/communism/football is my religion'. It is not uncommon to hear any one of these subjects called 'religion'. (We are reminded of Martin Luther's words, 'whatever the heart most desires is your God'.) The list does not end there and we are entitled to be confused as to what elements, if any, distinguish a subject as 'religion'. An RE teacher could have nightmares in trying to cope with an ever-expanding list. Some people think that if one is 'good' (an 'honest' citizen) then one is 'religious' (cf. 'he's a *real* Christian'). If it emerges from such ordinary views that there are grave misunderstandings in society about what a religious person, a Christian, Muslim, Jew, or Hindu, is, then a teacher of religion might well be concerned to get clear on the nature of the phenomenon we call 'religion', if only to himself, in order to make sound judgements, and so on.

The search for meaning in human experience is largely a question of coming to know more precisely what we judge an experience to be *of*. Determining that an experience is one thing rather than another involves some sort of demarcation between experiences. Not all who bow their foreheads to the ground are Muslim; not all who pay their taxes are Christian. An understanding of the world arises precisely by means of a grasp of generally accepted criteria. For instance, if we want to get a grasp of what 'sin' means we may ask, what are the *necessary* features of this concept? And we shall doubtless discover that at least one of the

8

criteria is the idea of 'separation'. This sort of thinking applies to religion as a whole. Thus the question 'What should we teach in RE?' requires some investigation into the nature of religion. But even before marking out boundaries there is the prior question of whether a religious *knowledge* (as opposed to mere 'belief') is important and, if it is, what sort of knowledge would that be? In other words, we wish to know if there is anything we can say is *true* in religion, just as, in history, we can say it is true that William won the Battle of Hastings. Of course, we may not want to discuss the question of knowledge and truth-claims in the classroom, at least not with pupils much below the age of 16. But we would certainly expect teachers to recognize what might constitute ways in which these claims may be made. For one thing it can be of enormous help in stating teaching objectives. Again, some idea of the answer will help us to decide, for instance, the relevance of the bible in teaching religion, or whether it is appropriate to bring alcohol and drug problems into our RE lessons, and if it is, then from what angle these problems should be approached.

It is not difficult to imagine people, parents and teachers, saying 'We can *prove* what is taught in science, mathematics and history, but the so-called "religious knowledge" taught in RE can only be believed', with the implication that RE is not therefore very important to education, perhaps even a waste of time. It has been argued by some that religion is not a fit area of study for public examinations on the grounds that religion is a private matter, to be understood only in 'personal' terms. On the other hand, if education is considered as a systematic development of the rational mind, and religion is to play a part in this development, then we ought to be clear on the sort of knowledge religion involves and its role in the educational process. The significance of the knowledge component in education had been discussed by, among others, P. H. Hirst. 'Knowledge', he says, is not 'something which the mind may or may not possess . . . To be without any knowledge at all is to be without mind in any significant sense' (Hirst, 1974a, p. 24). If Hirst is correct then we ought to have some idea of what the difference may be between 'belief' and 'knowledge'. Teachers of religion will not want to be continually justifying their subject as a 'respectable' part of the curriculum. They will wish to regard RE as no less a candidate for the part it is to play in the development of the rational mind than other subjects.

Since it is common to hear people speak of 'belief' in religion and to contrast this with 'knowledge' in, say, science, let us consider the two sentences 'I believe in God' and 'I know there is a God'. Clearly the second sentence is a claim to know something in much the same way as 'I know there are countless stars beyond ordinary vision'. The sentence 'I believe in God', on the other hand, carries with it certain normative overtones. That is to say, we have come to associate the 'religious believer' with certain attitudes and actions characteristic of the practising religious person. We think of the religious believer as being *committed* to certain attitudes and actions. We see a direct relationship between his belief and his behaviour. We may say that the believer binds himself to certain courses of action because of his beliefs. If someone tells us 'I believe in God' we usually have some expectation about his commitments and behaviour, and it is this expectation that obscures the fact that the sentence is also a claim to *know* something. For the statement necessarily presupposes, at least, that God exists. While it is true, therefore, that there is a difference between the two statements in terms of what we expect to follow from them (that is, in behaviour and attitudes of the religious believer as compared with the behaviour and attitudes of a person who simply makes a claim to know something), there is no difference between them that would enable us to describe one as a claim to know something and the other as a claim to 'only believe' something. They are both claims to know something, whatever else is involved.

Nevertheless, there is still something strange about someone saying 'I believe in God but am not religiously committed'. D. Z. Phillips puts it like this: 'If I say "This is the true God, but couldn't care less" it is difficult to know what this could mean' (Phillips, 1965, p. 149). We intuitively want to agree with Phillips. But what makes it important to pick out from 'belief' the knowledge or propositional component is our concern with education (while Phillips's concern is with elucidating a purely theological position). For while it is entirely appropriate to speak of religious belief in everyday life or in theological discourse as being connected to some form of commitment, in compulsory education we must be prepared to encounter, and perhaps even to engineer, situations in which claims to religious knowledge can be made and examined *without* consideration of personal commitment, or at least without any subsequent commitment becoming part of the educational process. For education is no longer concerned to proselytize its pupils but to bring about an understanding of what can be known in religion.

Formidable arguments have been advanced in an attempt to show that religion cannot be justified as a form of knowledge and that it is therefore incapable of telling us anything about the world. The charge of nonsense has been made against the possibility of religious knowledge, notably by philosophers of the 'logical positive' school of thought. Positivist criticism is sometimes characterized by the formula 'Every statement must belong to one of three categories. It is either (i) analytic (as in mathematics and formal logic); (ii) synthetic (as in science); or (iii) metaphysical (as in religion).' In the thinking of A. J. Ayer, if a statement cannot be verified in ways appropriate to (i) and (ii) then it is metaphysical and, as such, is 'neither true nor false but literally senseless' (Ayer, 1936, p. 31). But, as Norman Malcolm points out, our ordinary use of the word 'know' cannot always be understood in a 'strong' sense (Malcolm, 1967, ch. 5). Malcolm illustrates the common use of 'know' in this way (pp. 72–3):

> A great many people have *heard* of various theorems of geometry, e.g. the Pythagorean. These theorems are a part of 'common knowledge'. If a schoolboy doing his geometry assignment felt a doubt about the Pythagorean theorem, and said to an adult 'Are you *sure* that it is true?' the latter might reply 'Yes, I know that it is'. He might make this reply even though he could not give proof of it and even though he had never gone through a proof of it . . . He did not absolutely exclude the possibility that something could prove it to be false. I shall say that he used 'know' in the 'weak' sense.

Then there are other ways of showing religion to be a quite rational way of viewing the world without recourse to explanation by means of purely empirical investigation or mathematical deduction, as required by those who would insist that there are only these two ways of 'knowing' something to be true.

R. M. Hare thinks it is simply a mistake to talk about proof of God's existence as though it were an explanation for what happens in the world. (For example, it is mistaken to argue, from the fact that we can see order and organization in the world of nature, that therefore there must be a Designer we call 'God'.) It is a mistake because 'we no longer believe in God as an Atlas' (Hare, 1955, p. 101). Therefore whatever the world is like – including evil and suffering as well as love and joy – the religious person will still believe in God. What makes the difference between the believer and the unbeliever is the undisputed fact that they see the world in different ways. No amount of empirical 'evidence' *can* refute belief in the existence of God.

Perhaps Hare's way of showing that we can talk rationally about religious claims is disturbing to some. We may want to insist on the question 'Surely there must be a way of attaching religious statements to the 'real' world if they are serious claims to truth?'. Possibly we feel like this because of a well-established fiction. The fiction is that if we can touch, see, smell, hear, or taste something then it must be 'real' in a way we think we understand. But there is an important truth lying behind this implicit assertion that we can only know what the five senses tell us. It can be illustrated by the ordinary sentence 'Oh, I see what you mean'. This is interesting because we do not mean 'see' at all; we mean 'I understand'. If we now ask the question 'Which of the five senses is being referred to here?' we realize how inappropriate the question is. It is not appropriate because in saying we understand something we are doing nothing that can be immediately tested by the senses (given that the objects being experienced are agreed upon by all in the conversation). However, in saying 'Oh, I see', we have made a significant step forward in our knowledge, as when we say 'He's not just a dog; he's a friend', or 'It wasn't the aspirin that killed him; he died of a broken heart'. Our understanding if what we see, in other words, does not always or necessarily depend upon new information presented to us through the five senses. There is sometimes more in dogs than mere dogginess and we do speak of 'broken hearts' seriously. Hare draws our attention to the *different* ways in which we may understand the world even when all the 'facts' appear the same to everyone.

The idea that we see the world in different ways, even when the facts remain the same, is put forward by a number of philosophers. John Wisdom argued, in his essay 'Gods' (1953), that when two people are looking at the same picture it is not a question of the facts when one of them says the picture is ugly and the other that it is beautiful. Their disagreement cannot be settled by reference to the facts. The facts cannot decide the issue because they are all known to both viewers who still 'see' the picture differently. It may be true that if a picture tells its viewers something then it can be properly described, as John Casey has said, as 'a form of knowledge, but knowledge of something other than fact. Works of art do not provide us with new information' (Casey, 1973, p. 80). For Wisdom's viewers there is a knowledge to be obtained from the picture but it does not consist of more factual information than that which both viewers can already see. R. K. Elliott (1973, pp. 102–3) says:

> It may be that a work of art is precisely the kind of thing which calls for imaginal and personal response. One might say that that is its essence and life, and that the objectivist aesthetic extols not the work itself but its husk or corpse.

The religious person might be inclined to say that the purely historical or 'objective' observer (if such were possible) sees in the world only Elliott's 'corpse'. In seeing our picture of the world it is not just a question of whether we *may* see the facts in one way rather than another; we really do see one picture rather than another, for our view is not new information as to the facts already presented but new knowledge. To recognize the painting as either ugly or beautiful is, in both cases, to know something more than the lines that are drawn. And there is the possibility of settlement in our disagreements about Wisdom's picture, although differences 'cannot be resolved . . . by moving the picture but by talk perhaps' (Wisdom, 1953). A similar analogy can be made with music. We may hear certain sounds but only some people, not all, will understand the sounds as 'music'. No logic and no empirical test situation can tell us that the sounds are 'music'.

Decisions on what can be known in the world, then, appear to depend to a large extent on whether we can agree in our judgements; and the way we use language has an important part to play in the decision-making process. According to Ludwig Wittgenstein, the language we use is the building material of knowledge.

> 'So you are saying that human agreement decides what is true and what is false?' – It is what human beings *say* that is true and false; and they agree in the *language* they use. That is not agreement in opinions but in form of life . . . If language is to be a means of communication there must be agreement not only in definitions but also . . . in judgments. (1958, ss. 241 and 242; original italics)

We can never experience someone else's pain; but by using agreed forms of language a person with toothache can get us to understand almost exactly the experience he is going through. Since human beings have in common a multiplicity of experiences – including those of artistic expression, moral awareness and religious consciousness – and since these experiences can be expressed in a common language by which we are able to convey to others, more or less accurately, the nature of these experiences, then the road to a knowledge of what is true and false at least appears to be open, according to Wittgenstein.

Yet it may still seem strange at first to think of human knowledge as something that can only be 'known' by some form of 'agreement in judgments'. We tend to feel more secure if what we claim to know can be physically checked against one or more of our senses, regardless of what others think. We want to ask 'What are the *facts*?' as though 'facts' cannot be refuted. R. Pring says: 'That we distinguish between cats and dogs may be due to certain social conditions; that we *can* so distinguish has something to do with cats and dogs' (Pring, 1972, p. 25; original italics). However, although knowledge has to do with 'cats and dogs', the precise relationship between 'cats and dogs' and our *knowing* (consciousness of) their being 'cats and dogs' remains opaque. As Michael Oakeshott (1933, p. 42) says:

> Fact is what has been made or achieved; it is the product of judgment. And if there be an unalterable datum in experience, it certainly cannot consist of fact. Fact, then, is not what is given,

it is what is achieved in experience. Facts are never merely observed, remembered or combined; they are always made.

Put another way, a fact is not something like a dog that can be empirically observed in an obvious way. A fact is, rather, a statement concerning what is believed to be observed.

What, then, might constitute the kind of objectivity we feel we have the right to expect of 'knowledge' – and especially of religious knowledge? How can we escape mere subjective assessments of what the world, including 'religious' experience, is like? At least part of the answer, according to Peter Winch (1958, p. 32) consists in establishing standards.

> Establishing a standard is not an activity which it makes sense to ascribe to any individual in complete isolation from other individuals. For it is contact with other individuals which alone makes possible the external check on one's actions which is inseparable from an established standard.

In other words, we can recognize 'truth' in language by setting a given statement against a background of already established statements. This is not to say that objectivity is simply to be derived from a democratic vote. What Winch and Wittgenstein seem to be saying is that those within the 'agreement' situation must have some understanding of what the subject under consideration might mean, and its significance within the universe of a publicly accepted language. Since, however, a theory or idea which aspires to objectivity, especially in highly complicated forms of knowledge, cannot always be held up for independent assessment by people 'in general', the question of competence in judgement must also be considered. Yet it is also argued that we simply cannot go beyond our thoughts of what the world is like – and therefore beyond the language we construct for those thoughts – to find what we suspect is external to them, for even what is conceivably discoverable 'out there' is in the first place *conceivable* – and therefore part of the world *as we see it*. 'No', says Wittgenstein, 'experience is not the ground for our game of judging' (1969, s. 131).

It seems that while objectivity cannot be identified with truth there is an intimate connection between them. D. W. Hamlyn points out (1972, p. 107):

> inter-subjective agreement acts as a kind of linking-point between truth and understanding. For understanding what we mean presupposes agreement on the application of our terms at certain points, and agreement equally constitutes the criterion of the concept of truth.

If we are not to fall into solipsism then criteria for what is true and for what can be known of experience may be determined, in the words of Wisdom, 'by talk'. And if *that* is true then the teacher of religion has grounds for believing that his subject is no less 'respectable' in terms of the possibility of being able to make claims to knowledge in religion than the subjects of history or literature.

Having looked at various ways in which religion can lay claim to some form of objective knowledge we are also in a position to see the sort of opposition that the RE teacher might offer to those who claim that 'religion' has no more reason for being on the school timetable than 'magic' and 'astrology'. For while magic and astrology may continue to be regarded (at least potentially by some) as ways in which we can know the world, we do not have reason to suppose that they constitute a *religious* form of knowledge. This will be even more clearly seen when we come to discuss the sort of concepts it is appropriate to recognize (and therefore teach) in religion.

Distinctions and Contours in Religious Knowledge

What we have seen so far is that there are grounds for thinking that religion contains genuine 'truth' components, that there is a religious way of knowing something about the world. For obvious reasons this is of importance in secular state schools where a premium is put on the development of the rational mind and upon knowledge which constitutes a central characteristic of mind. However, although it is arguable that there are criteria by which one may claim to validate religious knowledge in a general way, we have not so far considered views that would mark out any specific religious elements. On what sort of grounds could we decide what is and what is not 'religion' between, say, Islam, communism and football? Sometimes people object to the idea that religion can be distinguished in any clear way. They say: '*That* is what religion means to you; but *I* think religion is something quite different.' We may observe at once that this statement already admits that there is at least something distinctive about religion, otherwise it could not be a serious claim to hold a different view. The objector will have reasons for his claim to hold a different view; he will have, at least by implication, criteria by which his view can be distinguished as 'religion'. But it is precisely because there exists the possibility for determining how best religion may be characterized that there is the possibility of agreement. What may make such an agreement *difficult* – though not impossible – is the vagueness of the views held. It will only be possible *always* to object to a certain characterization if we do not begin the dialogue that may lead to agreement. The subjects of history and ethics are also difficult

15

to characterize with any precision, but we would not wish to say that history and ethics defy characterization and that is all there is to be said on the matter. So how might one go about making distinctions that are of practical value to teachers?

P. H. Hirst's analysis of the forms of knowledge required in a liberal education may be used as a starting point. By a consideration of Hirst's thesis teachers are given a chance to apply rational procedures to a subject that is notoriously woolly. Hirst considers the grounds on which a 'liberal' education might be based, and construes such an education as one which has breadth and which, at the same time, limits that breadth to certain logically defined 'forms of knowledge'. The limitation is imposed, according to Hirst, by the nature of knowledge itself. A pupil who comes to know certain crucial elements in the contents of those forms is, accordingly, 'liberally' educated. Hirst sees it as necessary to establish criteria by which those forms may be identified. That done, contents to be taught will be relatively well marked out. The teacher's problems after that will be those of selection of material, determined by the criteria for the specific 'form' being taught, and the teaching methods to be used, according to the age and ability of the pupils.

Hirst's thesis (Hirst, 1974a, ch. 6) purports to describe the world of experience as it actually exists; he portrays it in terms of the concepts and propositions of a public language which are 'testable' by those who use that language. 'The conceptual and logical analysis which indicates the divisions I have stressed is a matter of the logical relations and truth criteria to be found at present in our conceptual schemes' (p. 92). Hirst's 'forms of knowledge' are not fixed in the Platonic sense. They are capable of development in principle. 'Being rational', Hirst continues, 'I see rather as a matter of developing conceptual schemes by means of public language in which words are related to our form of life, so that we make objective judgments in relation to some aspect of that form of life' (pp. 92–3).

Hirst distinguishes some seven 'forms of knowledge'. These are: mathematics, physical science, moral knowledge, literature and the fine arts, philosophy, interpersonal (or 'mental') knowledge and religion. 'The labels that I have used for distinct forms of knowledge', says Hirst, 'are to be understood as being strictly labels for different classes of true propositions' (p. 87).

The distinctive character of the various forms of knowledge is determined by (i) certain concepts unique to the form and not reducible to any other form (we may, as Hirst does, refer to these as 'categorial concepts'); (ii) 'these and other concepts that denote, if perhaps in a very complex way, certain aspects of experience, form a network of possible relationships in which experience can be understood' (p. 44; following Brent, 1978, p. 101, we may refer to the 'other concepts' as 'substantive concepts'); and (iii) objective tests peculiar to the form and by which its statements can be validated against experience as claims to truth. Hirst's approach is not to be confused with those of R. M. Hare or John Wisdom and other philosophers of religion for he does not set out to try to *prove* that there exists religious knowledge. Rather, he takes experience as evidence indicating that there probably is such a domain of knowledge, just as he sees what appear to be domains of knowledge in mathematics, science and aesthetics. His concern is to show that *if* there is a form of religious knowledge – as there seems to be – then it will be established as such by reference to its distinctive categorial concepts, its complex of substantive concepts and the way in which it can be tested against experience. The value of Hirst's thesis is that it enables us to identify as 'religion' those different human experiences that seem to point to religious claims as claims to knowledge and truth. And the virtue of his criteria is that they help us to distinguish religion from other forms of knowledge. Hirst does not attempt to *demonstrate* that religion is a form of knowledge; he shows the conditions it must satisfy *if* what we claim to be religious experience is legitimately to be so regarded.

Let us try, briefly, to apply Hirst's thesis to the religious form of knowledge in order to see what implications it can have for teachers of religion. Since we have already looked at ways in which religion may be 'validated against experience' (or 'made objective'), let us now work out some of the implications of the categorial and substantive concepts necessary to establishing the nature of religious knowledge.

The categorial concepts 'provide the form of experience in the different modes' (Hirst and Peters, 1970, p. 64), while the substantive concepts give substance to, or fill out, the distinctive area of a mode of experience. But substantive concepts, while necessary to the form as a whole (since they are what we most often directly experience in the world), are dependent upon the categorial concepts for their distinctiveness as part of the form. For example, in religion, of the concepts 'God', 'the transcendent' and 'grace' we would pick out 'grace' as a substantive concept for it denotes a significant and recognizable religious experience but does not *determine* the form of religious knowledge. Hirst would probably say that 'grace' constitutes part of the 'content' – the internal complexity – of the form. Only in relation to the concepts 'God' and 'the transcendent' can 'grace' be categorized as part of the religious domain of knowledge. 'God' and 'the transcendent', therefore, are categorial concepts marking out religion as a distinctive form of knowledge; the concept 'grace' can only be seen as a *religious* concept in relation to them. 'Grace' *presupposes* the categorial concepts, although it may be *through* an experience of 'grace' that one may recognize the categorial concept 'God'. In simpler terms we may say that our knowledge of God comes through an experience we have of the world commonly described as 'grace'. 'The specific forms the tests take', says Hirst, 'may depend on the lower level [substantive] concepts employed' (Hirst and Peters, 1970, p. 64). Together, the categorial and substantive concepts of the religious form of knowledge constitute the concepts central to that form.

If what has just been said were to be accepted, then a grasp of the interrelatedness of religious concepts would become essential for the RE teacher. Let us probe a little further. Some study of the major world religions shows marked differences between them in areas such as ritual, doctrine and organization. One might think of Christianity, Islam, Hinduism, Judaism, forms of Buddhism and animism in this connection. One item they appear to hold in common, however, is a belief in some form of 'the transcendent' or 'God', where this is taken to mean something like a supernatural experience or an intelligent 'spiritual' force acting in the lives of men and often focused in a being or beings describable in anthropomorphic terms. What is significant about this common concept 'transcendence', for present purposes, is not merely its commonality but the way in which it binds together all the other aspects of a given religion. For example, much of Hindu ritual (and therefore much of the organization of thought and practice in Hinduism) becomes meaningful only in relation to its various forms of deity. To take a specific example, Hinduism is *determined* by the injunctions of Lord Krishna in at least certain of its essential forms: 'For the man who forsakes all desires and abandons all pride of possession and of self reaches the goal of peace supreme. This is the eternal in man' (*Bhagavad Gita*, 2.71–2). It is not unimportant to know that 'ritual' is sometimes indistinguishable from everyday 'secular' practical life; in Hinduism 'a vast majority of the economically poor Hindus approach God through traditional simple methods using the ways of devotion (bhakti) and of performances (karma) rather than the path of pure knowledge (jnana)' (Sen, 1961, p. 20). There is a parallel with Christian practice here. For many Christians throughout the world religion is not at all intellectual but is practised in distinctive forms of devotion in church rituals and attitudes towards other people. The words of James's epistle seem to justify such attitudes: 'Pure religion and undefiled before God and the Father is this, To visit the fatherless and widows in their affliction, and to keep himself unspotted from the world.' Such practices would be regarded as religiously meaningless without implicit or explicit reference to God. In Hudson's words, 'The concept of god determines what in religious belief constitutes (a) an *explanation* and (b) an *experience*' (Hudson, 1974, p. 16; original italics). The concept 'God' determines, in a similar manner, all religious thought and practice in Islam and in other religions.

Within Hirst's forms of knowledge theory, then, the concept 'God' or 'transcendence' constitutes the categorial concept in the religious form of knowledge; all other concepts connected to religion are substantive concepts and depend for their specifically religious meaning on the

categorial concept. In order to bring out this relationship more clearly
we shall consider some of the substantive concepts with special reference
to Christianity.

Besides the concept 'God', Hirst, for example, mentions 'sin and
predestination' and in his critique of Hirst's theory Brent picks out 'sin'
as well as 'God' and 'the transcendent' as categorial concepts (Brent,
1978, p. 104). In what sense could 'sin' be regarded as categorial? The
scriptures and Christian tradition are quite clear on its use. 'Sin' means
breaking God's law; the state of sin is the human condition of being
alienated from God. There is no obvious sense in which it could be
claimed that 'sin' determines what religion is. 'Sin' denotes an act or
a human habitude *towards* God; this is its peculiarly religious meaning,
and without the concept 'God' the New Testament term for 'sin'
(hamartia) could be used in a purely secular way such as breaking the
law of the land or, more simply, to fail in one's purpose. Similarly with
'predestination'. It is difficult to conceive of 'predestination', as a *religious*
term, independently from the concept 'God' for within the context of
the Christian tradition 'predestination' presupposes the power and will
of God in the sense of there being something determined by God in
a conscious and designed act of will. The concepts 'sacrifice', 'baptism'
and 'salvation' all presuppose the concept 'God' in the sense that
statements involving these concepts imply notions such as sacrifice *to*
God, baptism *in the name of* the Lord and salvation *wrought by* God.
Thus 'sin', 'predestination', 'sacrifice', 'baptism' and 'salvation', and
other concepts such as 'ritual', 'worship', 'resurrection', 'paradise', 'the
day of judgement' and many others are substantive concepts in that they
presuppose the concept 'God'. Whatever state of affairs is called
'religion', and contains no concept of transcendence or its equivalents
and no terms which presuppose it, is religiously incoherent. Any concept
which does not necessarily presuppose the transcendent is reducible to
one of the other forms of knowledge. As Hudson claims of Wittgenstein's
'pictures': 'The fundamental pictures in the case of religion are . . .
pictures of god; that is, they express some aspect of transcendent
consciousness and agency' (Hudson, 1974, p. 21). A comment by Brent
is illuminating: 'Consider what will happen', he suggests, 'if the modern
attempts of the "death of God" school of theology at categorial revision
are successful and a coherent and recognisable system of *religious*
knowledge and experience is produced in which the concept of God is
redundant. The structure of the religious form of knowledge as a whole
will be transformed by altering the categorial concept of God' (Brent,
1978, p. 112).

If we accept Hirst's theory then the criteria for what we should teach
in RE are fairly clear. One important corollary for RE teachers might
be a renewed interest in the scriptures of all faiths. For Judaism, Islam

and Christianity the Bible is a major source of substantive concepts all dependent upon and shaped by the concept of God. The bible *uses* history to depict God; a secular bible, for the believer, is a contradiction in terms. A religious form of life, as Wittgenstein might have expressed it, is constructed out of our agreement on the concept of transcendence. To reduce this concept to something else, to some other form of knowledge, would be to claim that there *can* be no religious form of knowledge. The RE teacher should seriously consider this alternative.

Summary of Chapter 2

To be able to speak of religion as a form of knowledge and truth, as opposed to 'belief', is important for educational purposes because we regard the world of knowledge as a valuable part of what we want children to learn. A purely empirical or 'positivist' view of knowledge is inadequate since knowledge and truth are determined in significant respects by the language we use and the judgements we make about experience. By applying Hirst's thesis concerning the nature of knowledge it is possible for the RE teacher to work out a curriculum in religion that would satisfy the demands of a secular society and further the development of the rational mind.

★　★　★

3

Is It Meaningful to Speak of the 'Religiously Educated' Person?

Apart from its contribution to the way in which we can come to identify and to validate religious statements, Hirst's thesis has another function. The 'forms of knowledge' analysis is the result of a prior problem for Hirst: 'What is the nature of a general, liberal education?' The argument goes something like this: if the education of our young people is not to be unduly influenced by pressures of local moods, fashions, politics and mores (some might describe deliberate pressures of this kind as 'social engineering'); if pupils are not to be moulded in one specific way, as potential industrial manpower, for example, taught in schools for the purpose of their future utilitarian value in society; if, instead, young people are regarded as independent centres of consciousness, to be given all the help possible to develop as autonomous decision-makers; then the ultimate basis for education lies in its ability to offer young people a knowledge and understanding of the world that is as far as possible objective, free from prejudice and doctrinaire views and constantly open to revision. A liberal education (it might be said) is to be constructed from all those areas of knowledge that, while arising from man's own experience of the world and therefore to a degree subjective, become objective and independent of sheer locality by means of agreed, public judgements. The next step is to try to identify the logically distinct forms (if there is more than one) of knowledge that presently exist. The final step is to teach at least the chief characteristics within each form. We could describe this as constituting a general education in which the pressures of 'socialization', of political indoctrination, of moral and religious persuasion and of employment 'usefulness' are kept to a minimum in the interests of the person as an individual who may wish to keep his options open. (And, it might be argued, it is *desirable* to do so in the interests of developing the child's autonomy.) Now, if we accept

21

the value judgement on which this notion is based, namely, that education should be general or 'liberal' and objective, then the RE teacher may raise the question of the 'religiously educated' person. Let us, here, review three alternative ways of describing the 'religiously educated' person; not as recommendations but as descriptions introduced to highlight the problems that can arise from the phrase. The 'religiously educated' person is: (i) a person who knows a lot about religion; he is well informed about the function of religion in society; he can distinguish between different belief systems; he will be aware of whether he himself is religious or not; (ii) a committed religious believer whose knowledge of religion determines how he is to understand the world and how he himself is to function in the world; (iii) a person who studies religion, among other areas of human experience, but whose knowledge of religion can only be 'oblique' because religious statements are either not in fact known to be true or cannot in principle be known to be true.

The first alternative raises the question of whether it is meaningful to speak of being 'educated' in a single field of knowledge and we shall return to it at the end of this chapter.

It could be said that the thinking behind alternative (ii) represents an important standpoint among certain groups within contemporary religious education. 'All education rightly conceived', says the 1924 Cambridge Agreed Syllabus, 'is religious education.' This might be described as a 'total paradigm' in which all that is said and done in education directly relates to a religious view of life. Although alternative (ii) incorporates some of the characteristics of what Working Paper 36 calls 'The "confessional" or dogmatic approach' (Schools Council, 1971, p. 21) the dogmatism is muted and the 'confessional' aspects are disowned in contemporary literature. Instead, choices are offered, even if these turn out to be choices within the paradigm. The second alternative can be illustrated by examples from Islam and Christianity. Speaking of Islamic jurisprudence, Abdul Qader Audah (1971, p. 54) says:

It would be quite feasible for Muslim jurists to take hold of the sentiments of this [illiterate majority] group and guide it towards the right way, if they [the educated minority] but convince them that all matters in this life are related to Islam, and that their belief is never complete unless all secular affairs are treated on the basis of, and according to, Islamic jurisprudence.

A little later (pp. 58–9) the same writer says:

Some of those who received European education . . . have been affected so thoroughly by their studies that they believe the

European model is applicable in any country and under any social order. If they would apply their mental faculties more astutely, they would easily discover that the institutions initiated by men, including the system of European education, cannot be given precedence. Rather, the Islamic doctrines itself [*sic*] is what must be taken as the final word.

Thus law and politics are to be interpreted and administered by reference to the Qur'an and the *sharia* (a detailed code of conduct). With special reference to medical science, the Qur'an is cited in support of Islamic attitudes to knowledge:

> From the very beginning, Islam encouraged the pursuit of science and favoured progress. The precepts of the Quran and the injunctions of the Prophet bear testimony to this favourable attitude of the Islamic religion. Thus we find in the Quran: 'O my Lord! advance me in knowledge' (xx: 114). 'But those among them who are well-grounded in knowledge . . . to them shall We soon give a great reward' (iv: 162). (Aga Khan and Zaki Ali, 1944, p. 11)

Riadhe el-Droubie (1978, pp. 161–2) makes the 'total paradigm' clear:

> Islam is the religion in which there is no place for what is known as 'religious' or 'secular' areas of life. It takes life as one unit [encompassing] the entire field of human life . . . the whole concept of education is based on religious education as the foundation of moral conduct and practical living; that is why learning is placed on an equal footing with worship in Islam.

Educationists in the Christian tradition who appear to advocate the total paradigm of alternative (ii) claim, for example, 'that human life has a religious dimension and that religious *questions* are inescapable' (Smith, 1975, p. 69). A concern for 'truth' and refusal to 'ignore the ultimate mystery of death . . . might restore the religious dimension of human experience to a central place in the thought and life of the school' (ibid., p. 73). 'Religion and education *ought* to be one.' The New Testament concept 'agape', which 'awakens gratitude and trust', Smith suggests,

> might be acceptable to all who share our common humanity and who are prepared to acknowledge the power latent in the Christian moral tradition. Both might help to restore wholeness to human living . . . But wholeness can only be restored to the educational

curriculum by teachers who have found – or are committed to
seeking – a measure of wholeness and integrity in their own
thinking and living. (ibid., p. 74)

Smith comes very close to the often discredited 'confessional' teaching
of religion, but his position is modified by his recognizing that even
humanists may contribute to religious education. 'A true humanism may
reject religious answers but acknowledges the importance of religious
questions' (p. 72). To be educated, it seems, is to be religiously educated.
How could such thinking be justified in our education system? One way
would be to regard religion as a form of morality. No need, one might
say, to argue specifically Muslim or Christian doctrine but to see both
– as well as other forms of religion – as one logical development of
the moral life. The argument might run thus. The moral life is the
objective of education; those things taught in educational situations are
necessary elements involving the living of the moral life. The various
'subjects' – history, literature, mathematics, science – are the 'sinews'
of life; while the moral life itself, whatever makes life worth living, its
objectives, is the brain, the guiding faculty of existence; that which gives
life meaning such as cannot be obtained merely by the pursuit of
individual subjects learnt or employment undertaken. Religion in its
separate, distinctive forms is a development of that moral life. This is
a possible justification for the total paradigm. But it is not necessarily
acceptable to those Muslim and Christian educators who advocate the
total paradigm in a different form. For one thing, the argument reduces
at least the teaching of religion to the teaching of morality in one of
its forms; Muslim and Christian protagonists, on the other hand, would
perhaps argue that their morality depends for its validity on distinctive
religious doctrines, such as are set out in certain Qur'anic and biblical
commands.

The moral rationale is not the only one possible for those who seek
a 'religious' total paradigm. It is widely advocated that education should
reflect the structure of society in certain of its informal 'religious'
attitudes and values. Britain is nominally a Christian country, it might
be argued, and the education it offers should show this in appropriately
less formal ways, however difficult or against the grain this may prove
to be. Thus the 1975 Birmingham *Agreed Syllabus of Religious Instruction*,
while accepting that 'everyone should . . . recognise that education for
life in Britain today must include an adequate treatment of Christianity
as the faith which has, historically, moulded British life and culture',
goes on to say: 'whilst in some respects religious education is the task
of the specialist teacher, in others it is woven into the pattern of
community relationships. The whole life of the school should be one
in which the mind can be enlarged and moral responsibility exercised'

(Birmingham, 1975a, p. 7). Such a view apparently justifies immersing pupils in the traditional cultural values of British society, and the accompanying Handbook *Living Together* suggests how pupils might learn about and take part in organizations such as the 'Birmingham Young Volunteers', the Visiting Service for Old People, the WRVS, hospitals, cubs and brownies. This is indeed a more diffuse form of 'religion' but no less a total paradigm for that. The hard fact that teachers will also have to accommodate, compromise with, humanists and Hindus does not alter the argument, for humanists and Hindus are not representative, it will be said, of the national culture and the traditions to which the nation is still attached. The Muslim will argue along similar lines – with greater success, no doubt – in countries like Pakistan and Iran.

What may incline us to be sceptical about (ii) is that a total paradigm for the 'religiously educated' person seems to exclude certain genuine options. The 'believer' may see nothing strange in this. Others may wish to question the ability of this form of RE to lead the next generation to develop patterns of thought which will allow or even encourage alternative and non-religious views. A liberal education surely cannot presume to pre-judge a student's later commitments. Much of the thinking in what has been called 'implicit' RE may also fall into the total paradigm alternative. We shall consider the implicit approach in a later chapter.

Those who advocate the 'religiously educated' person of (iii) will not merely tend to be indifferent to the notion of religious commitment or, more simply, the teaching of religious beliefs but, in placing emphasis on 'reason' and the 'development of the rational mind' in education, will regard with open suspicion any form of religious teaching that may conceivably lead to commitment. 'What cannot be part of education, however,' says Hirst (1974b, p. 84),

> would be seeking to develop, say, a disposition to worship in that faith, or certain emotions of love of God, when that very disposition, or these emotions, are only a justifiable development if the religion is accepted by the individual. That acceptance I have argued is a personal, private judgment which education, committed to reason alone as it is, has no right to foreclose.

The alternative to teaching for such dispositions is to teach 'about' religion, says Hirst, 'provided that is interpreted to include a direct study of religions, which means entering as fully as possible into an understanding of what they claim to be true' (Hirst, 1974a, p. 187).

In his strictly utilitarian view of education Robin Barrow says: 'religious instruction lessons, even if they do not overtly assert the religious truths in question, may serve as a means to indoctrination, by taking it for granted that the religious subject matter is straightforwardly factual' (where 'indoctrination' is seen as 'the intentional implanting of belief so that it will stick, by non-rational means'; Barrow, 1981, p. 150). But 'it is entirely in order to study religions or a particular religion, perhaps historically or merely with a view to learning more about them, considered in isolation . . . But . . . imposing a long-overdue ban on the practice of teaching religion, should not be confused with an attempt to prevent teaching about religion' (ibid., pp. 150–1). The reason why we cannot 'teach religion' but only 'about religion' is, for Hirst, a consequence of the fact that no one has *as yet* shown adequate tests for the truth of religious statements; for Barrow it is that even if religious propositions have some intelligible meaning they are 'unprovable'. The more profound difference between Hirst and Barrow is that while Hirst includes religion within the concept of the liberally educated person, on the grounds that religion is at least a potential form of knowledge, Barrow speaks of a 'long-overdue ban on the practice of teaching religion'. Both Hirst and Barrow would agree that religious statements may be examined by the RE teacher, but only as beliefs that other people hold. On these views, then, the 'religiously educated' person is not merely one step removed from his subject matter but cannot be educated in any sense of the word 'religious', for the tendency (more strongly in Barrow than Hirst) is to reduce RE to, say, a study of psychology or sociology. If this line of thinking were correct then Hirst's inclusion of religion in the 'forms of knowledge' theory would turn out to be inappropriate and Barrow's ban on RE, as the teaching of *religion*, is not so much overdue as unnecessary.

Certainly RE would be suspect if it were the case that teachers took it for granted 'that the religious subject matter is straightforwardly factual'. But a major issue in contemporary RE thinking is to indicate ways in which religion and religious knowledge are not and never have been 'straightforwardly factual'. In this sense Barrow dismisses too lightly an area of experience which may well bear comparison with subjects he says are 'vital elements' in education such as English, history and philosophy (ibid., p. 140). If such a subject comparison can be made then Barrow, with Hirst, would have to take religious statements (true or false) seriously and include religion on any curriculum that claims to form the basis of a liberal education. We shall see in Chapter 6 that to speak merely of teaching 'about' religion is unsatisfactory.

We may contrast Hirst's and Barrow's conclusions and arguments with those of Ninian Smart. Let us pick out some four points made by Smart in his *Secular Education and the Logic of Religion* (1968) which seem to oppose the Hirst/Barrow view of the 'religiously educated' person.

26

We should be alert to the rationalistic devaluation of religion which is over-intellectualistic . . . There is no need for suspicion and compromise if it is but seen that the essential interests of different positions coincide, and that the logic of the situation demands an open treatment of issues of faith and history. (pp. 103 and 105)

On the basis of this evaluation Smart's first point is that while 'religious studies should emphasize the descriptive, historical side of religion'; it is also necessary 'to enter into dialogue with the parahistorical claims of religions and anti-religious outlooks' for 'there is a chain of logic from the empirical study of religion to the parahistorical' (p. 106). The empirical approach is 'descriptive' or 'historical' and can be equated with Hirst's and Barrow's teaching 'about' religion; but the term 'parahistorical' refers 'to those studies and arguments which concern the truth, value, etc. of religion' (p. 13). These elements, too, it seems must be included in the studies of the religiously educated person.

Questions of religious truth, whether truth has simply and supposedly been presented in revelation, or whether it has been discussed philosophically or otherwise, have traditionally been important in education, and it is therefore vital that we should have some notion as to how one arrives at parahistorical truth . . . How do we arrive at truth here? (p. 20)

And the methods of arriving at answers in this area are 'part of the methodology of theology' (p. 15). Barrow certainly, possibly Hirst, might balk at the thought that the 'religiously educated' person would have to undergo such studies. 'There are', says Smart, 'educational disadvantages in separating out too closely historical from parahistorical approaches to the subject' (p. 93).

The second point of contrast with Hirst and Barrow (whom we may say represent the 'descriptivists') is Smart's assertion that 'the essence of education is teaching how' as opposed to 'teaching that'. Although Smart is primarily thinking of the dogmatic teaching of the church – 'that God was in Christ and so forth' (p. 95) – his opposition to the idea of teaching 'that' could certainly be applied to the descriptivists, where 'teaching that' would involve purely descriptive accounts in which information 'about' religion is alone allowed. 'But education and learning transcend the informative. Should religious education not likewise do so?' Teaching 'how' is of at least equal importance. 'The person learning learns how to do something: he learns a skill' (p. 95). 'Religious education could be designed to give people the capacity to understand religious phenomena, to discuss sensitively religious claims' (p. 96). While specifically rejecting 'evangelizing', Smart argues that there must be created 'certain capacities to understand and think about religion' (p. 97).

Since 'education is teaching how' as well as 'teaching that', we may identify Smart's third point of contrast with descriptivists as 'the production of a ripe capacity to judge the truth of what is propagated' by religion (p. 97). 'Whatever one's standpoint, there can be little doubt that a sensitive appreciation of religious and ideological issues is important in education' (p. 105). 'Before agnosticism, there should be sympathy for faith. Before faith, there should be sympathy for unfaith' (p. 103). But for Barrow, the ability to 'judge the truth' of religious claims, however sympathetically, is precisely what is not possible, for such claims are 'unprovable'.

The fourth element in Smart's thinking must surely be a thorn in the side of all descriptivists, for commitment 'is implicit in the argument I have used about the necessity of the parahistorical approach to religious studies, even where the primary concern is the historical, that commitments should be encouraged to express themselves . . . Real commitment is as willing to listen as it is to speak', and is not to be confused with 'the bad sort of prejudice: it does not involve distortion: it does not involve lack of sympathy for other positions. It is not that crass evangelicalism which wants to find fault in those who do not agree' (p. 98). We shall later examine the notion of commitment in more depth in an effort to discover whether it is indeed relevant to religious education. Meanwhile there does seem to be substance in these views of Smart as we have opposed them to Hirst and Barrow in particular and to descriptivists in general. But it is instructive to ask, is the contrast between Hirst and Smart so great in the light of Hirst's further comments that 'pupils can only understand any religious position if they begin to grasp its concepts and therefore its truth criteria'? And, Hirst continues, in teaching 'about' religion one must 'include a direct study of religions, which means entering as fully as possible into an understanding of what they claim to be true. This will demand a great deal of imaginative involvement in expressions of religious life and even a form of engagement in these activities themselves', provided that such involvement does not mean 'asking pupils to engage directly in any religious activities for the sake of these activities themselves' (Hirst, 1974a, pp. 188 and 189). Would descriptivists wish to deny that 'parahistorical' questions of truth and value should be asked? After all, it is a truth of Christianity, for example, that the crucifixion of Jesus, whatever historical significance that may have, is without religious meaning if it is not directly connected to the ideas of sin and salvation. These and other doctrines in Christianity must therefore be taught, in a depth appropriate to the age and ability of the pupils, within the context of lessons on the crucifixion. The questions involved are, perhaps, not logical ones but questions of procedure; can we have enthusiasm on the part of the teacher without evangelism? Would descriptivists reject Smart's claim that education 'transcends the informative' or that the skill 'learning how' should be acquired by the student in order to develop 'the capacity to understand religious phenomena'? And, in spite of Barrow's assertion that 'the basic propositions of religion are unprovable', would descriptivists seriously wish to prevent pupils acquiring 'a ripe capacity to judge the truth of what is propagated'? The problem of judging the truth of religious statements lies at the core of contemporary descriptivist criticism of RE. Smart can hardly be brought to task for asserting that RE teachers should produce a 'capacity' in their pupils to determine religious truth, and this is sufficient to deny Barrow's epistemologically doubtful retort that religious propositions are 'unprovable'. However, there is a big difference between investigating truth-claims and making the assumption that there are truth-claims to be investigated. Smart does not help to dispel criticism of RE by ignoring this distinction. It is a matter of public record that 'confessionalist' and 'neo-confessionalist' teachers of religion speak as if truth were necessarily to be found in religious statements. A more significant difference between Smart and Hirst arises, arguably, in their different presentations of the nature of religion rather than in their views on what the 'religiously educated' person should look like. We shall examine more closely Smart's definition of religion in Chapter 4.

Alternative (iii) does not seem to be a satisfactory way of describing the 'religiously educated' person, then, on the grounds that the phrase is too ambiguous as to what is being claimed for it. Perhaps enough has been said to indicate some of the difficulties inherent in an attempt to describe the 'religiously educated' person. We might seriously ask at this point whether it is profitable to seek a dichotomy between the 'religiously educated' person and the 'educated' person; for it is hard to see how one can be 'educated' in one area alone of human experience, which is why we may consider alternative (i) to be unsatisfactory. We find ourselves looking not so much for a needle as for a straw in the haystack because the 'bottom line' is an inquiry into the nature of religious education; an investigation into the nature of those aspects of and attitudes towards religion whose characteristics best fit into the educational enterprise seen as a whole. Is the phrase 'religiously educated' merely a misleading description of what we want to say? We asked earlier how we would react to the phrase 'atheistically educated' or 'criminally educated', for there are bodies of knowledge and skills attaching to these descriptions, too. A significant distinction can be made, it was suggested on page 22, between 'religiously educated' and 'religious education'. The distinction seems to be that 'religious education' is part of an ongoing process of becoming educated while the phrase 'religiously educated' implies a course of completed training in a narrow range of skills. Now while it can be sustained that 'training' has a part to play *within* 'education', we no longer wish to use the word 'education' to describe the individual processes of knowledge and skill acquisition that go towards it – which is why it seems odd to speak of the 'atheistically educated' or even the 'musically educated' person. It is, at best, a loose way of describing how different subjects contribute to the process of education.

The phrase 'educated' applied to religion alone, therefore, is a somewhat misleading way of saying that there is a certain distinctive body of knowledge and skills in the religious experience of man that is to be acquired as part of a person's education. Seen in this way the difficulty in understanding the phrase 'religiously educated person' (remarked by Alan Harris, see page 4 above) is dissolved. The RE teacher is concerned to produce not the 'religiously educated' person but a person whose education has included a study of religion.

Summary of Chapter 3

We have briefly examined three ways in which the phrase 'religiously educated' might be understood. All three alternatives are found to be unsatisfactory. The total paradigm of alternative (ii), discussed first, is unsuitable because, whether from religious or moral motives, it would tend to circumscribe, and perhaps actively to discourage, the study of religion in a completely open and critical manner. Alternative (iii) is inadequate, we saw, because of an *a priori* doubt it casts on the truth value of religious statements and because of a tendency to emphasize only what others believe to the detriment of what, in fact, may be known.

The description of the 'religiously educated' person of alternative (i) is considered vacuous because it adds nothing to the concept of education that is not already stated or implied in the idea of a liberal education. It does, of course, mention certain aspects of content in a person's religious knowledge, but the knowledge component alone, of any subject, is not sufficient to justify the label 'educated'. We are led to conclude that the phrase is redundant and that the substance of it is more properly to be incorporated into the wider concept of a liberal education.

*   *   *

30

4

Theories of Religious Education

I

THEORIES CONCERNING THE NATURE OF RELIGION IN EDUCATION

In an introductory book of this kind it is impossible to do justice to all that has been written on RE in recent years. However, certain aspects of the subject stand out from among the hundreds of articles and books published. We shall examine critically the more important issues discussed. RE theory may be divided into two categories. The first places emphasis on the *nature* of religion as this concerns education; it sets out to study the question of how religion may best be characterized for educational purposes. To outline this perspective we shall consider, first, the so-called 'phenomenological' approach as this is represented by Ninian Smart. Secondly, there is the view that RE forms part of the subject matter of moral education and in this connection we shall look at the work of John Wilson. A third theory, that of Raymond Holley, holds that human nature is essentially 'spiritual' and that all pupils are therefore potentially 'religious'.

The second category of theory stresses the *function* of religion in education. This is a more instrumental approach and, either implicitly or explicitly, suggests how religion may best be taught with a view to the *use* of religion, its practical value to pupils.

Smart's theory, briefly set out in *New Movements in Religious Education* (Smart and Horder, 1975), brings together two aspects of man's experience that can be construed as 'religious'. There are, first, 'religions' in the 'traditional and conventional sense'. Examples Smart gives of this form of religion are Christianity and Buddhism, and the term 'explicit religion' may be applied to 'traditional' religions. Smart distinguishes six dimensions within the religions. They are: (1) doctrine, (2) myth, (3) ethics, (4) ritual, (5) experience and (6) social aspects. (Smart first elaborated these dimensions in his *Secular Education and the Logic of Religion*, 1968.) Secondly, there is 'religion' in a wider sense involving the depth of meaning in life. 'Questions about ultimate meaning that can be regarded as religious are to do with *values*' (Smart and Horder, 1975, p. 18; original italics). But it is the depth of the values involved that determines whether a value is religious or not, 'it is a matter of degree of depth . . . not just the limit of ultimacy, whatever that is, but near there, for the truly important questions of value also can raise religious problems' (ibid., p. 19). To strengthen this point Smart adds, 'though all value-questions have in principle a religious aspect, in fact it is more practical to see the deeper value-questions as religious' (loc. cit.) The term 'implicit' religion is used to describe the 'deeper value-questions'. 'Explicit' and 'implicit' forms of religion together constitute a fully characterized picture of religion.

Smart goes on to draw several important corollaries from this characterization. The six dimensions that we can discern in world religions are also features of some ideologies and Smart makes the parallel with Maoism in particular and Marxism in general which have 'sufficient resemblance to make it profitable to make comparisons'. Thus it is possible for Smart to conclude that 'the concept of a religion is non-finite in the sense that, surrounding religions proper, are certain secular systems of belief which somewhat resemble them. The study of religion needs to take account of these ideologies' (p. 16). Also, like the religions, ideologies purport to answer 'ultimate' value questions about human life. 'They may claim to be anti-religious but they are committed societies analogous to the Scotland of John Knox or the medieval situation of the Papacy' (p. 21).

In presenting the idea that 'implicit' religion arises in 'questions about ultimate meaning' and in 'deeper value-questions' Smart perceives the need for pupils to study 'values' in a general sense, albeit ' "ultimate" value-questions' and, more specifically, moral values. Smart suggests that we can distinguish a religious morality from a morality that is not religious by conceptually 'imposing' a religious interpretation upon moral actions. 'For example, if I wash up, I may regard this service to my family as a way of praising God' (p. 20). We may, similarly, 'superimpose' a religious interpretation on political ideologies where these concern life's 'ultimate' values (which totalitarian ideologies always do).

The characterization of religion as having both explicit and implicit dimensions has been influential in RE in recent years, and certainly reflects much of actual religious experience. In the second part of this chapter we shall look more closely at examples of RE in its 'implicit' form. At this point we shall confine our questions to Smart's definition of religion as he presents it in the six-dimensional form. Smart's approach has been called (for example, by Schools Council, 1971, p. 43; by Grimmitt, 1973,

p. 27; and by Holley, 1978, p. 171) a 'phenomenological' approach. The main characteristic of this style is to draw attention away from a confessional and dogmatic form of teaching religion and to focus instead on the various phenomena of religious experience in a more objective manner. 'The ideal teacher, in Smart's view', says the Schools Council Working Paper 36, 'is one who is ready to portray sympathetically and without bias any viewpoint which he may be required to teach' (p. 38). Holley says of Smart's analysis that it is 'a phenomenological description of overtly observable organized religious faiths, or communities' (1978, note 1, p. 171). According to Smart, therefore, we are to teach religion (in its definite and indefinite forms) from an impartial point of view and with a sympathetic understanding of the subject matter of the various religious forms − the 'parahistorical' approach that 'transcends the informative' (Smart, 1968, pp. 13 and 95).

The overall impression that we get from Smart's account of religion is that everything in life may have religious meaning if it is thought to hold sufficient depth of value. For the religious believer this is an unexceptional point of view. We may say that the believer has a religious 'world view'. But the teacher *as educationist* may ask a number of questions. For example, does the religious 'world view' mean that everything taught in schools has a religious perspective? For some the answer has been a decided 'yes', and in discussion and planning RE often falls under the heading of 'implicit' religion. There is a second and perhaps more searching question: is it appropriate for teachers of RE to regard the world as their oyster; to teach in such a way as to regard whatever is to be taught in schools as though it were 'religious' to some degree? If it is, then we may say that in one sense all education is religious education, reminiscent of the 1924 Cambridge Agreed Syllabus. If this does not sound absurd it is because we take it to be a view held by religious believers. Yet in a secular society which does not recognize that all that is taught in schools is in some sense religious we are left with the feeling that there is something odd about this particular line of thought. And the problem is raised that if it is the case that all education, for the believer, is religious education, then how is the teacher, *qua* educator, to avoid embracing the believer's view, and should he avoid it? Is it possible to teach religion in such a way as to confine religion to a distinctive and separate area on the curriculum, as with literature and mathematics? And would such teaching be satisfactory or appropriate for religion? (This is not to argue for 'subject' divisions and to suggest that there can be no interdisciplinary teaching in schools; but that concerns methods of teaching rather than subject matter.) More specific questions can, and need to, be asked of Smart's 'phenomenological' account of the nature of 'a religion' where this can be identified as 'religion in the traditional, conventional sense'.

Focus in complex experience is crucial to our understanding of the world. It is an inherent weakness in the phenomenological study of religion that it makes the *assumption* that religion is such and such, then proceeds to examine the phenomenon as though this were correct. We may surely agree that Smart's six dimensions are in some way involved in religious experience, but precisely *how* are they involved? Can they be said to characterize or define religion in any distinctive way? For example, we may all agree that 'doctrine' is a characteristic of organized religion, but it is not entirely satisfactory to say that 'doctrine' is necessarily of a religious nature. Christian doctrine, for instance, is very specific. The doctrine of, say, baptism has attached to it quite distinctive concepts related to fellowship with God and the salvation of man through the crucifixion and resurrection of Christ. If a 'Christian' were to believe that 'baptism' had no such connotations but was meant to signify a social position and future success in a particular social group then, while this rite might be accurately described as a 'doctrine' in some sense, it could not be a Christian doctrine. It is only partly true to say that Christianity is characterized by doctrine for without giving the doctrines of Christianity very specific meanings nothing of any *religious* significance emerges. If, on the other hand, we were to accept Paul Hirst's forms of knowledge thesis then a 'doctrine' or 'rite' could only be regarded as a religious doctrine or rite when directly related to some form of 'transcendence', 'god', or the 'superhuman'.

Take the 'ritual' dimension as a further example. 'Ritual', says Smart, is one of the six dimensions of a religion as well as of 'religion' in his 'implicit' sense. What is the logic that allows us to *deny* that certain rituals – say, smearing a fox's blood on someone's face – are religious? And by what criteria are we to assert that, say, sprinkling the blood of a lamb on someone's face *is* religious? Consider what happens when we bring into play Hirst's categorial concept 'God'. Smearing a fox's blood on someone's face has no reference to God but does signify, under certain conditions, an important occasion in the ritual of fox-hunting; it is therefore a ritual of one form of blood sports. On the other hand, sprinkling the blood of a lamb on someone's face, again under certain conditions, has a direct reference to the work of God in the Hebrew religion. Without that transcendent reference or criterion the act would have no clear *religious* meaning. We can say, therefore, that 'doctrine' and 'ritual' are describable features of organized religion; but without further consideration we cannot *assume* that it is *religion* that is marked out or distinguished. On Smart's view there are no criteria by which we can *determine* that 'doctrine' or 'ritual' is religious.

Smart's concern is to avoid a definition of religion that is too constricting, an aim with which RE teachers would wish to agree. But Smart does not say that *no* definition is required, for it is *as* a definition that he examines the six-dimensional model (Smart and Horder, 1975, p. 13). While it is

34

important to be aware that, as Smart says, religion 'has to be tied back to religion and religions as they manifest themselves' (Smart, 1970, p. 4), it is still necessary to ask how we are to identify phenomena as religious to begin with. Smart is, of course, aware of the problem of identification and explains the need for the RE teacher to include, in his descriptive and undogmatic approach, the *intention* of the believer; 'the meaning the activity has for the person or persons participating. It is strictly a misdescription if I say that a person is praying to a statue, if he conceives himself as praying to Vishnu' (Smart, 1969, p. 65). In adding this 'principle of intentionality' Smart deepens the study of the phenomenon in an appropriate way but leaves quite unsolved the problem of whether *what* is being studied is a *religious* phenomenon. We may say, therefore, that the dimensional approach advocated by Smart is rather to be seen as *a way of teaching* religion, but this can only be done after the process of identification has got off the ground. It is not only helpful for teachers to know what sort of animal they are dealing with in RE lessons; it is crucial if we are to fill the timetable with subject material appropriate to religion. We cannot say, merely by observing phenomena, what is typically religious, without prior agreement on what is to count as 'religion'. Acceptance of 'criteria' for what is to count as 'religion' does not, indeed, provide us with a 'rich account of the core of religion', as Smart observes (1970, p. 8), for that is not the point in picking out the criteria, but it does allow us to recognize the 'religious' in a way that detailed empirical study does not. The practical value for teachers of RE which Smart's six-dimensional account of religion has undoubtedly had in recent years should not be under-estimated. But it remains a necessary step to pin down the dimensions in a more precise manner.

Is RE one form of moral education? According to John Wilson, religion arises from the emotions which, in turn, are part of the field of moral knowledge. Emotions, argues Wilson, are connected to morality in the sense that morals concerns not only what people should *do* (behaviour) but also what people should *feel* (emotions). In moral education, Wilson says,

> We should want to assess people, not only by the kinds of reasons that motivate them, but by their general attitudes, feelings and dispositions; that is, not only by what they *do* (even if we include the reasons they have for doing it), but also by what they *feel*. (Wilson *et al.*, 1967, pp. 59–60; original italics)

From his list of 'moral components' by which we can identify the 'morally educated' person, Wilson emphasizes an 'ability', the 'awareness of one's emotions' (EMP 1), and 'awareness of others' emotions' (EMP 2) (Wilson, 1971, p. 261, ch. 10 and *passim*). This leads Wilson directly to religion for 'the notions of awe, worship, and reverence are perhaps *particularly* characteristic of the religious attitude'. It follows 'that it is not the type of *object*, but the type of attitude, which defines the activity we want to call "religious" ' (ibid., p. 42). Since moral education involves educating the emotions, and since certain of these emotions characterize religion, RE falls within the wider sphere of moral education. This, then, is the nature of the connection between 'religion' and 'morality', for Wilson. It could be argued that this connection does not result in reducing religion to the field of morals because, first, religion, for Wilson, clearly has a dual character in that while RE involves the teaching of those moral attitudes which have to do with the emotions, it does not deny to religion some form of transcendent origin based on statements of fact, rather than judgement. 'Worship', after all, has to do with an object towards which it is directed. 'Religion is *centrally* concerned with questions about the appropriateness of various objects of awe and worship, and with other human emotions' (ibid., p. 164). Secondly, by teaching the appropriate emotions only it is possible to 'elucidate a type of activity and belief which is *sui generis*, and cannot be assimilated to other activities, for example explaining, making moral judgements, stating historical facts and so forth' (p. 66). Since it is by means of the appropriate 'moral components' (e.g. PHIL, EMP, GIG and KRAT, cf. ibid., p. 163) that RE finds its logic, it is to be expected that the RE teacher need not confine 'his attention solely to those emotions, ideals or "outlooks" that may properly be called "religious" '.

> Religious outlooks are only one sub-class of emotion-based outlooks in general. We must include not only near-religions, like Communism or the Nazi movement, but (for instance) ideals like the ideal of 'honour' (not losing face), or 'Stoic' ideals of nobility and self-sacrifice, or 'Epicurean' ideals concerned with pleasure and a quiet life. (pp. 165–6)

RE, then, is a sub-species of the education of the emotions and of moral education, according to Wilson. 'It is not or not primarily, instruction in creeds, dogmas, sacred writings, history, literature, psychology, sociology or any of the other areas that have attached themselves to such emotions' (p. 186). We find Wilson a few years later emphasizing two important issues. The first is that of identification. At what point, he asks, do certain mundane attitudes become *sui generis* religious attitudes?

> We should be more inclined to describe Communism or Marxism as a religion the more that Communists and Marxists saw and described Lenin (or Marx, or whoever) not just as in a high degree important or admirable or outstanding, but as some kind of *god* – and 'god' implies 'something to be worshipped'. (Wilson, 1976, p. 21)

The second issue emphasized is the 'emotional investment' that lies at the core of religion. 'To *see* and feel Christ (Hitler, Poseidon, Nature, or whatever) *as god* – this element is central.' Mere history turns into religion when we go beyond the facts of the life of Jesus and portray him as 'divine . . . As soon as any specifically religious term is used – "god", "supernatural", "divine" and many others – we have to face the question of whether the attitude which these words incorporate is *appropriate*.' A person 'must be open to, or be able actually to feel, the emotions and attitudes which he might then want to invest or adopt' (ibid., p. 22).

Wilson's account of religion in education seems confused. Does he or does he not reduce religion to morality on the grounds that religious people express emotions? Is Wilson seriously saying that if emotion is expressed over an experience then such experience is to be understood in terms of the emotions? Let us, therefore, press the question: is religion logically linked to 'specifically religious' terms like 'god', 'supernatural', and so on, or is religion to be characterized by certain 'appropriate attitudes' within the autonomous field of ethics? The problem is resolved for Wilson by his assertion that we cannot 'step outside' the area of ethics (which, for Wilson, includes religion) without stepping inside one or more of Hirst's other forms of knowledge (Wilson, 1971, p. 163). We may make a number of observations. 'Religion' as '*sui generis*' is, for Wilson, clearly reduced to a form of morality; that is, religion is one form of moral thinking, namely, the association of certain emotional attitudes towards a 'divinity'. It follows that in teaching the 'moral components' in their entirety the teacher will necessarily be teaching, also, religion. What, then, of 'specifically religious terms' like 'divine', 'god', and so on? We are asked by Wilson to see that at a certain point mundane emotional attitudes become *sui generis* religious attitudes, and it is difficult to deny that this fundamental change appears to be brought about by the recognition of an object as 'divine' (that is, some form of 'transcendence'). In opposition to Wilson's former conclusion, therefore, to the effect that 'religion' is characterized by emotional attitudes, we may now observe that such a recognition of divinity is an *intellectual* transformation, and that this event – the recognition of an object's worth or significance – determines how we should characterize our feelings; it is not our feelings which determine what the object is. We are brought to characterize our feelings as religious by a recognition of the transcendent nature of the object. Thus the mundane emotion 'awe' which we felt when we first heard the roar of the erupting volcano becomes distinctively *religious* awe only when we come to believe that what we hear is the voice of God on Horeb. And if this interpretation is correct then no amount of educating the emotions will necessarily lead to religious understanding. Without a recognition of some form of the transcendent, the emotions will remain mundane. These two observations show the underlying inconsistency – the source of our confusion – in Wilson's thinking. We may conclude, therefore, that what determines the nature of religion, and therefore of what must be taught in RE, are what Wilson calls 'specifically religious' terms, not 'moral components'.

Wilson's emphasis on the pupil's actually *feeling* 'the emotions and attitudes which he might then want to invest or adopt' is also questionable. On the conceptual level, if a pupil comes to feel awe or reverence for an object thought to be divine (and this is apparently what Wilson means by 'appropriate attitudes'), does not this imply that the pupil must first come to believe that the object exists, that its nature is thus and so, and that it is worthy of reverence? And if this is correct, is not the teaching and learning of facts and concepts relating to the nature of the phenomenon logically prior to feelings of awe and reverence that may or may not be appropriate? This is also, surely, the way we teach music or art; and it would be just as inappropriate to claim that music and art are to be characterized by, and recognized by means of, the teaching of certain emotions. Wilson does, indeed, claim comparability between these subjects in terms of 'experience'.

> For teaching 'RE' is not a matter merely of instruction: the child also requires *experience*. In trying to educate children in those areas commonly called 'musical appreciation' or 'drama', we are not content merely to instruct them about music and drama: we also require them to take part in concerts and plays ... Provided we keep our aims clearly in mind, there is an obvious case to be made out for giving children that experience of religion that may be gained by particular forms of worship . . . Like other aspects of religious education, this falls into place once we realize that we are out to educate children in religion, not to inculcate a particular religion. (1971, pp. 175–6)

But we should not forget that the point about teaching music and drama is not that pupils shall become musicians and actors. It is that they shall come to know, to 'appreciate', what music and drama are; music and drama education is essentially a study of their nature and meaning, not necessarily, nor even centrally, playing an active part in concerts or drama. Where teachers require pupils to play a musical instrument or to act a part in a play it becomes one form of teaching method; a good one, perhaps, but not a logically necessary one. When we speak – as we often do – of getting pupils to 'experience' music, we do not mean that they must play musical instruments. Wilson appears to have confused two senses of the notion 'experience'. The first sense, getting pupils to understand and appreciate music by listening, by instruction, by discussion, and so on, is what teachers most often do and what is usually meant when we speak of teaching music in schools. This form of 'experience' is necessary in a logical way because it is what is meant by 'music appreciation'. The second sense, getting pupils to have an 'experience' of music, by playing an instrument, for example, may well be icing on the educational cake, but it is not necessary to a knowledge and understanding of music. It can be argued that engagement in an experience at the compulsory school level is an important part of teaching method, and therefore a means to certain ends; for methodology is not an end in itself. That end, as I shall suggest in Chapter 6, is to get pupils to understand, rather than to engage in, certain accepted forms of human experience. 'Sin', like 'god', is a peculiarly religious concept; what emotions would Wilson have pupils learn in order to achieve an understanding of this concept? Wilson's emphasis on a pupil's 'feeling' and 'experience' of certain emotions appropriate to religion, therefore, may be seen as an exaggerated (perhaps misunderstood) interpretation of certain teaching methods in RE, for he does at least make it clear that 'we are out to educate children in religion, not to inculcate a particular religion'.

One might ask whether the educating of certain emotions, for example, awe, worship and reverence, linked with the idea that pupils should come to 'feel' and 'experience' such emotions, might not actively promote a particular religious view of the world. How would one guard against that? And if there are religious believers teaching RE who would not object to such a result, would those same teachers be equally imperturbable when pupils are learning to understand and feel emotional aspects in communism, fascism, or the worship of Aphrodite (cf. Wilson, 1976, p. 23)? Perhaps there is a simpler answer to the suspected paradoxes implied in these questions. Wilson's stated reason for connecting religion with moral education is 'the feeling, now widely shared, that religious education alone could not provide a completely satisfactory framework for moral education' (Wilson *et al.*, 1967, p. 177). We would suggest that perhaps the reason why religious education could not, and still cannot, provide such a framework is because there was and remains an epistemological distinction between them.

Criticism of Wilson does not mean that the learning process in RE cannot or should not use the emotions as a means, a teaching aid, to the understanding of religion (although that would have its dangers). It is intended to indicate that we cannot assimilate RE to moral education by characterizing religion as emotion or by exaggerating the emotional experiences that religion undoubtedly involves.

More recently Raymond Holley has suggested that religion is essentially the 'spiritual' dimension in life and that the most important aspect in the teaching of religion is 'religious understanding' (Holley, 1978). What, according to Holley, is a 'spiritual' dimension? Three aspects of the 'spiritual' in life can be distinguished. First, there are features of physical life that are not entirely accounted for in terms of 'bio-chemical reactions and cause-and-effects events'. There is also the 'invisible and intangible in life' that finds expression in 'loving, feeling, hoping, perceiving, thinking, giving'. Secondly, there is the 'spiritual' that may be contrasted 'with the mental rather than the physical', in the sense that 'spirit' is 'ultimately that which is beyond strict, succinct' rational language. Human language only 'hints at rather than grasps the spiritual'. The third characteristic of 'spirit' (its 'most positive' aspect) is its 'restless energy, dynamic activity . . .' (pp. 49 and 50).

The spiritual dimension of the religious person, being itself 'non-physical' and 'unbridled by spatio-temporal considerations' (p. 57), 'implies the objective reality of the ultimate spirituality of the cosmos' (p. 59). For the Christian, this 'objective reality' is God, and the relationship between the religious person and God consists in man's abiding by 'ontological values'. In Christianity 'ontological values' include 'love, patience, mercy, pity, charity, sympathy, chastity and humility' (p. 108). Such values are to be distinguished from moral, social, aesthetic and intellectual values which properly belong to 'autonomous moral discourse'. 'Ontic values' determine all other values, including moral values, and are 'the final stopping points in any argument of an evaluative kind' (p. 109).

These two elements − the spiritual aspect in man and an objective spirituality of 'the cosmos' − lead Holley to a crucial issue in his thesis about RE. How is the spiritual in man able to reach out and understand the transcendent and objective spiritual of the universe? Holley argues that such a union can be made by the development of 'religious understanding'. The 'spiritual dimension of personal life' must actively engage in living the life of faith as this is exemplified by 'ontic values' (p. 106). Further, in order to provide adequately and appropriately for 'religious understanding' the teacher of religion must be aware of the difference that lies between 'religious understanding' and 'scholarly understanding'. Although 'religious understanding' and 'scholarly understanding of religion' are both 'intellectual pursuits', they have different objectives. Religious understanding 'is the handmaid of religious faith' and has a practical nature; while 'scholarly understanding of religion is entirely theoretical in its telos and intent' (p. 121). Religious understanding aims at an understanding of 'the-self-in-the-cosmos' such as the 'ontic values' demand. Scholarly understanding, on the other hand, using the normal tools of the scholar − those of the historian, the psychologist, the theologian, and so on − is one step removed from its subject, religion and the life of the believer. 'Religious understanding', says Holley, 'is logically prior to the establishment of any deep scholarly understanding of religion' (p. 125).

The task of the RE teacher, then, is to 'provoke' religious

understanding and 'sensitivity' to 'spiritual insight'. This is not to 'evangelize' or teach religion in a confessional way.

> A religiously educated person is one who is capable of spiritual insights as and when required, and who also has some scholarly understanding of religious phenomena . . . The religiously educated person is one who is aware of the spiritual dimensions of personhood . . . who realizes that personal fulfilment is not simply a matter of material possessions, meretricious academic advancement, social status and acceptability or political aggrandizement, but is a matter of spiritual growth and development which is to be achieved by clinging to ontic values. (pp. 142–3)

Finally, RE is not just one aspect of education but is the binding force in education and is central to the educational process as a whole. This is so, says Holley, because (a) 'religious understanding' provides 'unified insight' into every other way of thinking, and (b) it is the vehicle of communication between persons since there is always agreement 'in the spiritual dimension of life' (pp. 168–9).

Numerous questions spring to mind as we follow Holley's account of religion and the consequences this would have for the RE teacher. In the first place we might feel that although Holley's characterization of the 'spiritual dimension of the religious person' may be true of religious people, why should we wish to develop a 'spiritual dimension' in everybody else? Human beings commonly have tendencies – latent or otherwise – to violence (in self-preservation, for example) and evil (cruelty, for example), but we would not wish to develop these tendencies necessarily. Yet in other societies, past and present, they may seem laudable; they may be seen as desirable qualities of valour, strength, or pride. It is not obvious that we should try to develop qualities or potential powers in children just because the potential exists. Pupils are potentially many things. Some of them not nice. There are potential politicians, potential Marxists and presumably potentially religious pupils. Whatever potential – or lack of it – a pupil may have, we do not presume in general education to promote especially a potential of this kind, for there would be the possibility of 'provoking intellectual understanding of personal life' in objectionably restrictive ways. In teaching historical insight or mathematical skills in education we are developing qualities generally regarded as valuable. Is it not assuming too much of a secular society to expect it to value a 'spiritual dimension' so specifically connected to the religious life? Secondly, it is arguable that the 'spiritual dimension' as described by Holley does not exist. At most, it could be said, the sort of dimension Holley elaborates is little more than a sophisticated relic of primitive man's superstition; it cannot be taken for granted that religion and religious belief arises from a *natural* propensity in man for spirituality. It is quite reasonable to suppose the contrary: that spirituality has to be created and developed. And that, one might suppose, would be a task for the church, not the state school. It could be said that 'ontological values' like 'love' and 'sympathy' are, after all, no more (and no less) than part of human moral or social discourse. There would be, in that case, no difference between 'religious understanding' and 'scholarly understanding'.

We may, in education, wish to speak of 'religious understanding' and 'understanding religion' interchangeably. Let us take one example in order to illustrate the difficulty raised by the distinction Holley makes. Holley says that, among other things, (Christian) religious understanding means to grasp the idea that the statement 'God is good' is not part of 'autonomous discourse', but a 'declaration of the ontological nature of the spiritual ultimate'. It is one of the 'ontic values' to be recognized by the 'insights' of religious understanding. What we may ask is, in what way precisely can we *deny* this interpretation as 'scholarly understanding'? The fact that we may interpret a purported religious statement in one way rather than another is not sufficient for the claim that one way is 'religious understanding' and another is 'scholarly understanding of religion'. The test for 'truth' in religious understanding, according to Holley, is 'believing in, and pursuit of' values such as 'freedom', 'peace', and 'justice' when these are perceived as an 'authentic pattern of ontic values which constitute spiritual reality'. But is it so obvious that these values 'constitute spiritual reality' while other values do not? A Christian who rests his confidence in the list of virtues supplied by the letters of St Paul can afford to be dogmatic; but the RE teacher may well make it his business to call into question those values that seem so obvious to a Christian.

In his analysis of 'intellectual understanding' Holley is at pains to show that our understanding of 'objects', which includes values, is impossible without a publicly recognized use of language. From this it would seem to follow that scholarly understanding of religion, far from being *determined* by religious understanding, actually *constitutes* religious understanding, so far as this concerns the use of public concepts in a public religious education. (This is not to deny that in less sophisticated thinking there can be religious *perception* by the religious person; the point about this is that we may teach these religious perceptions by means of the normal tools of scholarship.) This line of inquiry allows us to conclude that the 'provocation of spiritual insight' may be provided by the properly trained teacher by means of his scholarly understanding of religion – provided we recognize that this may be seen only as 'confessional' teaching of religion.

If it can be argued, therefore, that 'religious understanding' can be reduced, in the educational situation, to simply 'understanding', that is to say, the teaching of pupils in such a way that they may reach an understanding of religion, then the task of the RE teacher is much the same as that of any other teacher, namely, the teaching of a subject in such a way as to bring about an understanding of that subject. RE is not, after all, the keystone of the education system.

II

THEORIES CONCERNING THE FUNCTION OF RELIGION IN EDUCATION

If much has been written about the nature of religion in education, far more has been said about the function of religion in schools, a mixture of content and method applied to religion as a curriculum subject. The task of differentiating between the approaches, the better to assess their meaning and value, is made more difficult because, over the years, procedure and content have tended to blend with one another and to hide theoretical assumptions that often lie behind them. Our task is made easier if we are able to identify individual strands of theory. Labels are a useful device for this purpose so we may begin by attempting to name the various processes used or advocated, remembering that the dividing lines are not always clear and that theories of the function of religion in schools often overlap. Since most of the labels have been in use for a number of years, and are not always used to describe the same function, I shall first describe what I think are the main features of each.

(1) *Confessional* RE means the overt teaching and strengthening of the Christian faith, its doctrines and way of life. It is the counterpart in schools to 'preaching' in Christian churches.

(2) *Neo-confessional* RE is, as the term suggests, the confessional approach with a changed style. The style is twofold. First, special attention is paid to pupils' mental and emotional abilities to understand religion within the context of the assumption that pupils will, eventually, accept a religious faith. Secondly, the neo-confessional approach allows 'open' debate and study of other religions, but only as 'tolerated extras' (as the Schools Council Working Paper 36, p. 30, puts it).

(3) *Hidden-confessional* RE appears to offer pupils a choice from among various religions. Confessionalism can be 'hidden' in the sense that it is simply assumed that a choice can and perhaps should

be made from among different religious beliefs; that there is a 'truth' to be found and that it is the teacher's task to help pupils to make a 'choice' from among these beliefs.

(4) *Implicit* RE involves the view that religion may be taught within any curriculum subject, for the emphasis here is on the view that 'religion' can be discovered in any area of human experience. It is also appropriate to examine under this heading tendencies to teach RE from the *believer's* point of view and problems that arise when, through a lack of distinction between a 'religious point of view' and the educator's view of religion, a large part of contemporary RE theory lays emphasis on the former. It is one thing for teachers to teach that religious believers have a 'faith by which to live'; it is quite another for teachers to 'stimulate the search for a faith by which to live' (Dorset, 1979, p. 14). The latter is arguably a function of religion, not of education.

(1) Confessional RE

It is easy for the 'liberal' educationist to decry the teaching of religion in a confessional manner. But it is more generous, and perhaps more helpful, to remember that Western education arose largely from a Christian religious environment. Thirteen hundred years of education in Britain cocooned in a Christian environment cannot, and perhaps should not, be lightly dismissed. We may remind ourselves that Christianity has been taught in previous centuries in much the same way as science, mathematics, or history is taught today. That is to say, religion was taught as a body of information and judgements about the nature of man and his beliefs in contemporary society that had to be passed on to the next generation. This form of teaching was and is unexceptional. What has changed in the past hundred years is attitudes and beliefs with regard to religion. The most important of these is an unwillingness by many to accept that a rational basis can be found for the claim that religion contains statements of true belief. It could be argued that similar changes have occurred in science. (We no longer believe that the earth is flat; we have revolutionary new ideas about a space–time dimension.) The difference between religion and science with regard to education appears to be that while scientific knowledge might change its appearance, religious knowledge is thought to have disappeared as knowledge. We speak now of scientific 'facts' much as we once spoke of religious 'facts', and where there appear to be conflicting views about the same subject matter there is a strong tendency to accept a 'scientific' rather than a 'religious' explanation. It is often said now that while one can hold religious belief one cannot have religious knowledge, and we have already considered the question of knowledge in religion. It should be clear from that discussion that the problem in confessionalism is not that claims to truth and knowledge cannot be made in religion but rather that teachers should not teach for religious commitment in pupils.

One might consider many of the Agreed Syllabuses up to the mid-1970s to be representative of the confessional approach. The *West Riding Agreed Syllabus* (1966, reprinted in 1969), for example, claims that there are certain 'personal needs of children' and that 'from the Christian point of view these personal needs are religious needs, which are only satisfied by the growing discovery that at the heart of the universe there is a God who cares, a Spirit who seeks to enter into personal relationship with us' (p. 3).

Many other RE publications have contributed to the confessional point of view. Richard Acland ends his influential book *We Teach Them Wrong* (1964, p. 191) with these words:

> If, by the time they leave school, the adolescents know that the Church is not asking them to believe the impossible; if they are not waiting for a 'Proof' . . . if therefore they stretch out in the hope of being aligned with whatever may be active at the heart and core of Life . . . is there not a fair chance that they will be found by the Truth of God?

To the confessionalist, therefore, the function of RE is to extend the work of the church into the schools; to bring young people to accept the Christian religion. It is only necessary to say here that whether or not true statements of belief can be made in religion, it is widely accepted that the work of the RE teacher does not involve the inculcation in pupils of a religious commitment. But we may ask how far this view is maintained in practice.

(2)   Neo-Confessional RE

The movement away from a confessional teaching of religion has been slow. Of the two characteristics in neo-confessionalism already mentioned – its emphasis on the need to consider the child's abilities, and some study of other religions – only the second hints at a development in the subject matter itself. It could be said that Ronald Goldman and Harold Loukes made, in the 1960s, outstanding contributions to RE by drawing the teacher's attention to the psychological and sociological difficulties of pupils in understanding the language and thought forms of religion. (See, for example, Goldman, 1964, 1965; and Loukes 1961, 1965.) Goldman concludes his research into the pupil's development of religious thinking by saying (1964, p. 246):

> it is hoped that this [book] provides a realistic picture of [the teacher's] pupils' development which will enable him to help the young achieve a deeper understanding of the Christian faith and a belief in God which is intellectually satisfying.

Loukes's conclusions direct attention to the centrality of biblical teaching in the formation of the religious believer (1961, pp. 151 and 152):

> In some such [previously described] vision of the Bible lies the only hope of restoring it to the place it used to hold, as a book that ordinary men are glad to read . . . If the work is well done, the young adult will take into his new life something in which he must believe and by which he must stand.

As Michael Grimmitt observes, for Loukes 'the "personal quest" becomes a "Christian Quest" ' (1973, p. 25).

The second element of the neo-confessional style is that which encourages pupils to study religion in a more 'open' manner. The Newsom Report says (Newsom, 1963, s. 163):

> However diverse the staff may be in their philosophical alignment all will approve of such positive well doing. Inside the classrooms, too, there is much common ground which Christian and agnostic may travel together. Christian ethics after all owe much to Aristotle as well as to Judaism . . . the whole staff, irrespective of religious affiliations, can make a united contribution to both the spiritual and moral development of the pupils.

Religions other than Christianity are suggested for study, but only in the context of understanding Christianity. Similarly, the Plowden Report (1967, s. 575) allows that

> During the last years of the junior school more specific religious education should be given, and, from such areas of the curriculum as history, literature, poetry, geography and music, discussion may arise which bears on religion and brings in judgements on values.

However, once again the context is within a framework of Christian faith and worship: 'They should be taught to know and love God and to

46

practise in the school community the virtues appropriate to their age and environment' (s. 572).

The 'openness' of approach in RE advocated by some writers does not, and does not pretend to, conceal a Christian religious confessional form of teaching, even where this could be described as non-dogmatic. While acknowledging that 'the idea of "teaching for commitment" is of course quite out, being an affront to the sacred principle of pupil autonomy', Colin Alves goes on to say:

> RE has been forced to abandon any procedures or purposes which might be labelled 'indoctrinatory', and as a result has been reduced to a vague exchanging of unchallenged opinion on matters of mainly ethical concern, or a purely academic study of the practices and doctrines of 'world religions' where Christianity only gets a brief look-in if it is lucky.

He continues: 'I recognize that there is "a potential possibility" that the educational enterprise in this country may break loose from the Christian roots which have so far fed and informed its growth. But I firmly believe that that time has not yet come' (Alves, 1972, p. 95). Finally, Alves cites with approval a passage from the *Cambridgeshire Agreed Syllabus* (1949) which, in part, says: ' "the God of Christian faith is a God who will have men to be his 'fellow-workers'. It is God that 'worketh in us both to will and to do': yet for that very reason we are to 'work out our own salvation' " ' (ibid., p. 124).

(3) Hidden-Confessional RE

A recurrent theme in contemporary RE is that pupils should be taught in such a way that they shall be able to 'choose' between the religions, often by means of a 'questioning attitude'. The confessionalism lies in the idea that there is such a choice to be made and that one of these 'choices' is true. What makes it 'hidden' is the assumption that there is a 'truth' to be found. Thus while stating in the preface to his *Religion and Secular Education* (Smith, 1975) 'a classroom teacher is not a religious evangelist', Smith actively encourages the religious attitude by claiming that 'Heideggar's most important contribution to the philosophy of religious education lies in his emphasis on the significance of death for human existence', for an awareness of 'mystery' – particularly the mystery of death – 'is the religious dimension of human life' and only the 'religious systems of mankind' can 'offer *answers*' (p. 50; original italics). Smith, therefore, emphasizes the importance of religious questions in RE since, as he says, 'traditional Christian belief, however brilliantly restated, is not a possible base for religious teaching in state

47

schools today' (p. 69). However, for Smith, the questioning attitude in a search for truth can only lead to a religious view of life. 'It might', he says, 'restore the religious dimension of human experience to a central place in the thought and life of the school' (p. 73). There can be no doubt, according to Smith, that the 'real' truth, the quest for which is the work of the school in general and the RE teacher in particular, is to be found in Christianity: 'We should try to deepen our pupils' insight into the central and enduring Christian theme of agape. The cross of Jesus symbolizes the depth of suffering which perfect love involves in a loveless world' (p. 122). While he is aware that the teacher is not a preacher, confessionalism – an implicit or explicit exhortation to pupils to acquire or strengthen a religious position – is for Smith the real driving urge behind RE.

Much the same could be said of Edwin Cox's views in *Changing Aims in Religious Education* (1966). Although Cox states that 'to look on religious education as aiming at conversion . . . is to put it out of line with present educational theory' (p. 63), he goes on to suggest that the RE teacher may present some form of religious belief as the objective of RE (p. 66):

> The Christian teacher can be assured that a non-evangelistic approach need not offend his conscience. If he is convinced of the truth of his religion, and that a thorough and sincere examination of human experience will lead to the decision that the Christian explanation of life is the most comprehensive and satisfactory, then he will be content to direct his pupils to that thorough and sincere examination, confident that by so doing he is advancing the Christian cause without the unfairness of hiding from his pupils that other ways of synthesizing experience exist.

And again: 'At the present time of uncertainty and rethinking it must be a search in which teacher and student "feel after truth and find it", as far as their experience and understanding allow' (p. 96). It might be considered that a marriage between a truly 'open-ended' RE and the search for 'truth' as it is presented in this context is likely to be entered into with a clause of divorce already written into the deed of union.

Edwin Cox has more recently produced *Problems and Possibilities for Religious Education* (1983). It must be said that Cox goes to some lengths to avoid the appearance of a confessionalist approach to RE in state schools. In *Problems* Cox presents a more clearly educational approach to the study of religion in schools. However, he still wishes to place emphasis on the popular view that a major function of RE is to assist 'the search for growing human beings for integration and for consciously held, adequate, directive values' (p. 134). Although such a view 'goes beyond a Christian, or even a specifically religious, framework', Cox acknowledges that such a 'conception of the subject has affinity with the Loukesian "implicit religious" education' (p. 135). Is there not, still, in this view a plea for us to think of RE as something superior to (or at least, 'different' from) other curriculum subjects? To make the assumption, as Cox seems to, that pupils *should* hold 'adequate, directive values' is not the same as teaching pupils the nature of 'integration' or values. Citing the White Paper that preceded the 1944 Education Act – 'the subject "should be given a more definite place in the life and work of the schools . . . to revive spiritual and personal values in our society and in our national tradition" ', Cox continues: 'That seems to have been lost sight of in the intervening years' (p. 113). This indicates that Cox has not entirely given up his earlier confessional-type approach. Moreover, does not Cox throw out the baby with the bathwater? He says (loc. cit.):

> If it cannot be argued that religious education should be taught because religion is true or popular or useful or cultural, then in order to justify it one has to show that it, and it alone, provides some other social understanding or personal knowledge that pupils need. That involves putting it in a wider educational context so that it is contributing, along with other learning, to the provision of a universal insight which all need to acquire in order to understand what life is about. Then it would be accepted as valid by all.

Is it indeed the case that we cannot show religion and religious statements to be true? And, whether they are true or not in a scientific or empirical sense, why should we wish to look for 'some other social understanding or personal knowledge that pupils need' other than that of studying and understanding the nature of religious phenomena, including its claims to truth? Why should such an objective study of religion *not* 'be accepted as valid by all'? As Smart has, rightly I think, pointed out, it is a sound educational procedure in studying Christianity to consider the arguments of Christian theology, and 'engaging with them involves raising questions about truth' (Smart, 1969, p. 63).

One reason Cox has for extending a study of religion *beyond* a study of religion is the view that RE ought to have a personal impact different in kind from other subjects studied. Unlike objectives in history, literature, or music in which the pupil is taught to know, to understand and appreciatively evaluate the meaning of the field at a point one step removed from himself, RE, according to Cox, should more directly guide the pupil's personal life. Thus Cox suggests that questions being asked at the secondary school stage should include, how do 'belief systems' help us 'to understand and develop ourselves?' since such an approach 'would be a more structured study of religions, strongly resembling the type of religious education that has been customary in the past' (1983, p. 138). On this view RE would resolve itself into a journey of discovery about *the pupils themselves*. (This is presumably what Grimmitt means when he says that a pupil in RE should 'learn from religion about himself'. See below, page 75.) One may well ask whether such an approach is some kind of counselling in moral and social behaviour rather than RE. The pupil's attention may be at first, on this view, directed towards objective phenomena, like music, Marx, or Muhammed, but rather sooner than later the subject becomes a dialogue with experience concerned with the 'purpose' of life, intended to evoke 'life's ultimate significance, its values, meaning, and purpose' in relation to a 'personal search for meaning' (Schools Council, 1971, pp. 43 and 19). It is at this point that 'hidden confessional' RE has close ties with 'implicit' RE, for both approaches now seem to offer, among other things, personal guidance towards some non-imposed but identifiable religious/value goal still bearing traces of the confessional tradition.

Two other characteristics in contemporary RE deserve closer critical examination. They may be called 'choice' and 'truth' in RE. Ideas such as the 'personal search for meaning', the answering of 'ultimate' questions, even the 'settling of personal qualms' all tend to represent RE as a supermarket in which choice has to be made; in which a way of life may be discovered. But the kind of choice considered in the literature, as we have seen, turns out to be whether or not students shall choose as a matter of personal belief to accept *this* set of doctrines or values, or *that* particular way of life. Within an educational context this aspect of teaching and learning seems inappropriate. What is the *educational* relevance, when teaching, say, the Christian concept 'baptism', in suggesting that a student may now choose whether to be baptised or not? If it be retorted by the teacher that such was not his intention but, rather, his intention was that the student should become 'aware' of the meaning of 'baptism', then such an explanation would seem to reduce to 'teaching the concept "baptism" ', a quite legitimate aim in RE. But it follows from this that, since 'baptism' is a central concept in the Christian religion, no 'choice' is possible; for coming to understand Christianity *means* learning the concept 'baptism'. By the logic of the situation students in school are not allowed to choose whether to learn or not what 'simple addition' means in mathematics. Similarly in the teaching of Christianity, there *can* be no choice about whether or not to learn the meaning of the most important concepts.

More generally, education, seen as a second order process, does not hold within its meaning that students shall choose to be this or that *within* the educational situation but, rather, that they shall be equipped for choices that may (or may not) be made ultimately and at a stage beyond the process. Choices and decisions of the kind envisaged by many writers and educationists in RE belong to the autonomous, educated individual, not to the student *qua* student. Education is, and ought to be, I have suggested, a comprehensive study of man's experience; but the idea of 'choice' indicated in the RE literature seems to lie beyond this study. There seems to be a difference of a logical kind between, for example, knowing what music is and being a musician; or, to use Oakeshott's imagery, between learning how to drive and being a driver (Oakeshott, 1967, p. 156). It might be thought self-evident that the logical difference consists, on the one hand, in undergoing an education which gives individuals the power to choose and, on the other, the act of choosing. As Peters has said: 'The pupil has gradually to get the grammar of the activity into his guts so that he can eventually win through to the stage of autonomy' (1964, p. 46).

Daniel W. Hardy (1979, p. 107) outlines a procedure for RE in which discussion can take place

> without prejudgements . . . and therefore allows that the truth is at issue between these [different religious] traditions and that it is that truth which is interwoven with the personal lives and views and actions of its adherents in the classroom. Hence religious education tries to foster open communication between truth-tellers in an atmosphere of mutual respect and trust. The supposition is that the truth is in such discussion and will emerge through this open communication.

The phrasing is odd when read in an educational setting; it might be more at home in the opening remarks of the chairman of some oecumenical church meeting. Why should it be assumed that even knowledge, let alone 'truth', exists among students in an RE lesson? And does any precise meaning attach to the idea that a 'truth' of some kind is 'interwoven with the personal lives and views and actions of' pupils? Is it of any educational moment that 'truth', in, say, science or history be so 'interwoven' with the lives of pupils? Does such a lack of proximity retard a pupil's understanding of, say, the biology of an amoeba or the campaigns of Caesar? What can be said about this 'search for truth' in RE? Direct personal involvement, engagement in a first order experience is clearly implied if not always stated. Consider, then, the idea that teaching religion involves a quest for 'truth', for it looks distinctly odd if it be compared with other subjects on a school curriculum. Would we normally say of a music lesson that we are looking for musical truth? Or of a mathematics lesson that we are seeking mathematical truth? It might be agreed that there is such a thing as truth in music (though it may be difficult to say what that might be) and truth in mathematics, and so on. But what seems to be odd in putting down 'the search for truth' as an objective in a lesson is that it is stated as an issue to be discussed or discovered *separately from* the subject matter itself. It is a logical oddity in that in, say, a physics lesson talk about the relationship between electrons and nuclei is what it *means* to talk about 'truth' in physics. Similarly in mathematics; the 'truth' involved in $2 + 2 = 4$ is the *same thing* as $2 + 2 = 4$. It is, simply, unnecessary to state both that the object of the lesson is 'to come to understand an equation' *and* 'to discover the truth about an equation'. Being able to say exactly what the truth is in religion may be at least as difficult as being able to say what the truth is in music, but nothing is added to a lesson objective which claims to 'bring pupils to a knowledge and understanding of the religious idea of salvation' by the further statement 'pupils will also look for the truth in salvation'. This is so because bringing pupils 'to know and understand' what is involved in the idea of 'religious salvation' will involve necessarily bringing to them also some notion of its 'truth' value within the discourse of religion. The precise point I am concerned with here is that comments such as 'at the present time of uncertainty and rethinking [RE] must be a search in which teacher and student "feel after truth and find it" ' (Cox, 1966, p. 96) seem to betray an extra-educational element, a desire to get pupils involved in religion as a first order experience, or in some non-religious experience such as the 'right' social attitude. None of this is to deny that epistemology, or a study of truth-claims, may be included in an educational process. Far from it. But this area of study is perhaps more appropriate to a course in philosophy, or it may at least be recognized as the *meta-phusis* of each form of knowledge. This simply takes us back to a consideration of whether, and by what criteria, religion may be regarded as a form of knowledge in Hirst's sense. A discussion of truth-claims in this latter sense is not the same thing as the idea of a 'search for truth' – or, more accurately, perhaps, 'a search for something to believe in' – as it is portrayed in contemporary RE literature.

(4) Implicit RE

What is 'implicit' religion? 'Explicit' religion has to do with the doctrines and practices of a traditional religion; for example, the Christian religion. Working Paper 36 says that 'implicit' religion might be, for example, 'the capacity to explore music with a view to seeing whether it can give one new insights into the nature of the world; and, if so, the connexion of these with questions about the "purpose" of life' (Schools Council, 1971, p. 44). 'What we have termed "implicit" religion', the Working Paper goes on (p. 53),

> may feature in discussion at almost any point in the school day, and teachers of many disciplines will be contributing, one

way or another, to their pupils' search for answers to religious questions. For example, a good biology teacher will be willing to discuss with the pupils their qualms about vivisection, even though this is not really part of the academic study of biology.

In using the term 'implicit' religion Working Paper 36 intends to draw our attention to the notion of integrated studies on the curriculum. This is part of the debate on methodology with which we are not especially concerned in this book. However, there is another way of understanding the term 'implicit' religion. It may be regarded not as a teaching method but as a religious believer's way of seeing the world. To the believer, it might be said (and this includes Muslims, Jews and Hindus as well as Christians), the whole world is a religious phenomenon in either an 'explicit' sense (where God speaks directly to man) or in an 'implicit' sense (where earthquakes or sickness may be regarded as a punishment). Problems become acute in RE when the notion 'religion' appears to exclude nothing; where social organizations of all kinds and theories of many hues — even anti-religious theories — are all thought to involve religious meaning, however tentative, however obscure they may seem to be. Working Paper 36 comments, surely correctly (p. 36):

To describe as religion any 'quest for meaning' in life, poetic insight, artistic vision, etc., which involves no necessary reference to any transcendent spiritual order or being for its interpretive principle is surely doing violence to language.

Let us consider the *Birmingham Agreed Syllabus*, together with its Handbook *Living Together* (Birmingham, 1975a, 1975b), as an example of a growing trend, and one might presume it to be a reflection of contemporary RE. The syllabus was something of a test case for the relevant section of the 1944 Education Act. In spite of protests the syllabus was not only accepted as 'legal' but seems to have established the 1944 Act (excluding the 'worship' clause) as a reasonable educational provision, according to John Hull, within which RE teachers might work in a multicultural society (see Hull, 1976, p. 35).

The first question we might ask concerns both the content of what is thought to be religious in the traditional sense, and the way in which this content is seen in the Handbook to be related to non-religious stances. For example, can it be reasonably maintained that the non-religious life-stances which the Handbook proposes for study in RE lessons actually constitute an education in *religion*? In his argument against the humanist

Dr H. Stopes-Roe, John Hull, citing the Handbook, says (Hull, 1976, p. 30; original italics):

> in addition, interest is being shown in many of the ideas basic to what have often been described as 'secular faiths'. In arguing for a Syllabus which will contain studies of Christianity and the other major world-faiths, the introduction continues 'Again, *on the same grounds*, other widely held stances for living . . . *require* serious attention in any realistic programme of education for life today.' Then we read, 'The other provisions (i.e. those dealing with the secular stances) are *equally important* for a *properly balanced* programme of work.'

This position is a source of confusion. It is a fundamental and consistent view of the Birmingham Syllabus that RE ought to include 'secular faiths' and non-religious 'stances for living'. One must press the question here, as against Smart, what is the justification, more precisely, for including what appears to be non-religious thinking in a study of religious thinking? The reply offered is that such non-religious thinking and stances for living 'require serious attention in any realistic programme of education for life today' and are 'equally important for a properly balanced programme of work'. But this surely misses the point. We have already seen that it does not seem appropriate for RE alone to concern itself with education for life *in general*, since that is, presumably, the objective of the whole education process. If the RE teacher be required to prepare a programme for 'realistic life today' in the more unrestricted sense then the teacher will be little less than a one-man education system. The difference between a whole course of compulsory education which might indeed be expected to prepare pupils for 'life in general', and a course in one part of that process, is significant. A 'religious' education which recommends for study so many major 'life-stances' (covered in sixty pages of the Handbook) is vast indeed. The objection concerns the implication that a study of *religion* involves, as a necessary part of its content, a knowledge of such a variety of human experience. John Hull, defending the syllabus, says that 'non-religions' are to be included in RE because they are 'deemed to be relevant to a thoughtful education in religion, and because any understanding of religion would be impaired which did not place the religions in the context of their great secular rivals and alternatives'. It is 'their very non-religiousness, their self-conscious offering of themselves as foils to religion, which made them interesting, relevant and educationally significant in a syllabus of religious instruction' (ibid., p. 32).

However, Hull's argument would be tantamount to the claim that, for an area of experience to be understood by pupils, it must *at once* be contrasted with other forms which are dissimilar in certain vital respects and only *in virtue of which* the experience itself can be seen to be significant, and without which a knowledge of the particular experience being taught would be impaired. Hull seems to be making the point that for something to be distinguished and understood it must be seen in contrast to something else. And this does seem to be the thinking of the Birmingham Handbook conference; as Edwin Cox says (1976, p. 126):

> The manner in which Humanism and Communism are treated in the handbook suggests that there are unsolved problems in including these in religious education. They are not included in their own right but to 'highlight the distinctive features of religious faith'.

It does indeed follow that to know that an object is, say, a tree is to know it is not, say, a house. But this obvious piece of logic is not an argument for the teacher of religion to become also a teacher of politics or non-religious · humanism, any more than a teacher of music must, in order to make the subject understood in its world context, immediately explain how music may be contrasted with art. Such a discriminating activity (and education may be characterized in large part as a discriminating process) is simply part and parcel of the process of education as a whole. That fundamental, conceptual differences between religion and, say, politics, do exist Hull would agree, for that is the point of words such as 'rivals' and 'contrast' which he uses. But is there sufficient reason to propose that it ought to be the teacher of religion who should teach also Marxism and non-religious humanism or local government or secular ethics for their contrast value? That they are all systems of belief does not disguise the fact that they are different in kind and centre on vastly different categorial concepts. In principle an RE teacher may just as well choose certain historical judgements or certain forms of literature to mark contrasts of belief. Perhaps it ought to be considered more seriously that to speak of communism and non-religious humanism as 'rivals', and to use them for points of 'comparison and contrast' in religious teaching, is to make them part of a teaching *method*. It is to use them in a particular way, as a means, not an end. And Cox is surely correct in commenting: 'if the study [of humanism and communism] is to promote understanding of a pluralist society they ought to be included in their own right' (1976, p. 126). There is nothing unusual or educationally unsound in using contrast as an educational procedure; but in this case it must be recognized that in using communism and humanism in this way they must be seen as peripheral and subsidiary to a knowledge of religion. Moreover, to recognize teaching in the areas of humanism and communism as pedagogical method in RE, that is, as a means to 'highlight the distinctive features of religious belief', does not seem to be consistent with Hull's remarks that non-religious stances are *'equally important'* and 'require serious attention'.

When Hull says, continuing his argument against Stopes-Roe, that humanism is not made 'unworthy or distorted' by this approach (1976, p. 33) he may, in the event, be correct but merely irrelevant since if, as has been suggested, literature or history might instead serve to show 'contrast', it would also be possible to use purely fictitious examples to 'highlight' religion. Indeed, Brent has done precisely this in his short science-fiction story of the 'black cloud' (Brent, 1978, p. 105). By means of this story Brent can make very clear distinctions between what counts as 'religion' and what does not. To use communism or humanism for their contrast value is not only not necessary; it may also be educationally suspect. Certainly it seems unlikely that Marx can be 'studied in his own context' and 'religions and the non-religions are on exactly the same footing' (Hull, 1976, p. 33), while at the same time these areas are regarded as a *means* to a knowledge of religion. Conflicting aims become mere confusions if we take seriously Hull's comment 'all are studied *as part of* religious education' (1976, p. 33; original italics).

My second main question relating to the Birmingham Syllabus concerns the persistent theme that 'religious education' is 'woven into the pattern of community relationships' (1975a, p. 7). The wording is peculiar. What might be said to be woven into the fibres of society is 'religion', not 'religious education'. The distortion of RE which, arguably, occurs in schools as a result of this misdescription cannot be helpful. To embark on a study of social life in Birmingham (or anywhere else) as part of RE is, quite simply, to confuse the issues centrally involved in forms of knowledge as disparate as psychology, sociology, history, religion, aesthetics, morality, and so on. On this score the distinctive form of knowledge 'religion' would be lost or diluted to the point where it could hardly be distinguished from social studies. Progress in knowledge (and therefore in education) is, as has been suggested, a discriminatory process in which we are able to identify the 'wood' by means of the 'trees'. If it be counter-argued that the aspiring citizen will have to live and work within such indiscriminate personal and social contexts and that preparation in state schools is therefore important, then it must be asked why it has ever been necessary to distinguish RE from all the other subjects taught, and why it is thought relevant to make distinctions between any subjects. Presumably it is the business of, say, the teacher of sociology to concern himself with such social phenomena as trade unions, leisure and the welfare state. Similar parallels can be made for teachers of science, history, politics, ethics, and so on. By itself, therefore, the argument that pupils need to know about certain personal and social phenomena does not support the case that it is the business of the RE teacher to bring this about. Religion is one 'tree' among many in the 'wood' of society; each one must make its own contribution from the specialist knowledge it has. What does support the case for having on the teaching team of a school a teacher of religion is the fact that there are features of society which are distinctively religious. And it is surely this teacher's task, one might suppose, to pick out those features of human experience which are peculiarly religious. If features in the individual and in society cannot be marked out as distinctively religious, then what, it might be asked, is the justification for the inclusion of a teacher of religion on the teaching team? If, on the other hand, there are distinctively religious features, then it is with these that a teacher of religion can be expected to concern himself.

Similar problems of demarcation arise in other Agreed Syllabuses and in much of the literature in the contemporary debate where 'implicit' religion is advocated. For example, 'the use of historical evidence' and how the 'human spirit' expresses itself 'through music and the arts' are topics to be found in the Dorset Syllabus of RE (Dorset, 1979); a study of the community, 'an introduction to its organisation', 'care for homeless children', 'old people and handicapped' appear in the Dudley Syllabus (1979). No doubt a case could be made for interdisciplinary studies among these and other areas mentioned. But this is quite another matter, as has been suggested, from the assumption that is made that a study of religion necessarily implies also a study of other autonomous or semi-autonomous disciplines.

In a 1979 radio broadcast Val Arnol-Foster caricatured RE in this way:

> The days of strict bible teaching have gone in all but a few denominational schools, to be replaced by the study of 'life-stances' (Marxism, etc.) and snippets of comparative religion. In the sixties they invented 'life-themes' for primary schools and 'problem-centred discussions' for secondaries. We heard a believable spoof of a primary class project on sheep . . . We're doing sheep, children, because they are mentioned in the bible. No Alistair, we are not going to do a project on boils.
>
> They didn't need a secondary school spoof. Instead they had a young RE teacher, gloomily teaching a syllabus that started with astrology and werewolves ('Things in their own experience') and probably ended with those lessons described by one pupil as being 'discussions of drugs, sex, violence and world poverty'. The bible has been replaced by a 4,000-book resource centre and teachers are so anxious about offending anyone or imposing anything that the pupils are learning less and less about more and more.

For teachers and writers concerned with RE, protestations that new syllabuses and ideas are now 'unbiased' or 'non-indoctrinatory' are not enough. Reasons given which seem to support the changes that have occurred are insufficient. The reason commonly given is that populations in the metropolitan world are not now 'Christian' alone but 'multi-racial', 'multi-cultural' and 'secular' with the differences of religious and non-religious experience this mixture implies. This will not do. The relevance of such mixed societies may bear a special relationship to methods and materials in teaching techniques within such changing societies, but this reason is not a satisfactory explanation for changes in the nature of religious knowledge. The only justifiable grounds for changing the content of what must be taught can be, obviously, only that the subject matter itself has changed. This does not yet seem to be the case in religious knowledge.

Perhaps the biggest single problem area in 'implicit' RE is that of ethics or moral education. Why is this thought to be a problem? In the first place, although ethics plays a large part in modern secular societies, no special provision is made for it on the school timetable. This in itself is odd until it is realized that moral education (ME) is generally inserted as a sub-heading in the RE programme. At least this large and important subject has houseroom there. But why, we may ask, in RE? The reason is probably historical. At the beginning of compulsory education in the West over one hundred years ago the only acceptable form of morality, speaking generally, was thought to be that enshrined in the distinctive tenets of Christianity. Therefore the RE lesson was also the ME lesson. But there is another complication. RE (involving ME) held, in earlier years, a different status from other subjects on the school timetable. Unlike subjects such as arithmetic and history, 'religion' (in this case Christianity) was taught as a confessional dogma; its principles were basically unquestioned and unquestionable. 'Religion' in schools was no less than an extension, an arm, of the church. The attitude of the teacher in religion was that of the preacher rather than the teacher. (It is still the practice, in some fee-paying schools, to appoint only ordained ministers or 'practising Christians' to the RE department.) Students were expected to become committed to a Christian way of life by means of the dogmas. Thus patterns of religious behaviour were also tenets of ME, for no distinction was made between them. Old habits die hard. We may ask whether it still is the case that most specialist teachers of RE are committed, practising believers. If this is so, is it not just possible that religious teachers of RE may have a genuine and deep desire to teach aspects of their religion as if such aspects were also 'moral'? Yet since we no longer regard RE as an extension of the work of the church; since RE is no longer regarded as confessional by nature, ought we not, now, to investigate the logic of the relationship that places a secular pattern of behaviour, namely, ME, within the purview of religion? For it can no longer be automatically assumed that a religious teacher of religion can or should teach secular patterns of behaviour (ME). The rationale that held together religion and morality a hundred years ago may no longer apply.

Indeed, in a secular society, it cannot be assumed that society's morality has anything to do with religion. *Prima facie*, therefore, it appears that a case could be made for distinguishing between RE (which will involve the teaching of religious patterns of behaviour – 'religious morality') and ME, which will involve the teaching of, an examination of, what the secular society regards as 'morality'. Some similarities in the material there will surely be, for today's secular societies were yesterday's committed religious communities. But teachers would at least be clear that in ME there is no necessary relationship with RE; and teachers of religion would no longer imagine that the religious patterns of behaviour they must perforce speak about have any practical and personal application in a modern secular society. Peter Gedge says of the 'implicit' approach to religion (1975, p. 51):

> If it is adopted as the sole approach to RE and ME, it may not do justice to a proper concept of RE, because it is too easy for the distinctively transcendent elements in religion to escape attention, and it might hinder a proper treatment of ME by assuming a theistic basis to morals.

In this connection it is useful to remember that for the Jew the scriptures are no more concerned with an autonomous man-reasoned moral code than they are with a purely historical account of the Hebrew nation or a scientific account of various physical phenomena. Thus 'Thou shalt not kill' is not part of a moral code having its metalogic in the sanctity of human life but is a divine command given for specific circumstances. (It does not forbid war, for example.) For Jew and Muslim alike 'secular scripture' is a contradiction in terms. Then there is the point that scriptural commands and injunctions, because they are of divine origin, effectively take moral responsibility out of the hands of the individual. The individual is not allowed to decide between good and evil without reference to basic religious commands. 'To obey is better than sacrifice', Samuel told Saul when Saul took it into his own hands to keep alive Agag, king of the Amalekites (1 Samuel 15: 22). Indeed, the whole idea of religious authority negates what Kurt Baier has called 'moral self-mastery'. 'Adults without moral self-mastery', says Baier (1973, p. 108), 'are not moral beings.' This is not, of course, to condemn the religious point of view, but merely to indicate a fundamental distinction that can be made between religious injunctions and secular morality.

If, therefore, 'implicit' RE means, as it sometimes seems to mean, that religion may be seen in many different forms of human experience, then there is the danger that we shall confuse two things: first, the nature of religion as it is seen by religious people and, secondly, what pupils may be *taught* about this. It is one thing to recognize that for the believer

59

religion embraces all of life; it is another for the RE teacher to formulate a teaching programme related to this religious view. The RE teacher may explain to his pupils how it is that religious people see the world in this all-embracing religious way; he may point to art, music, social organizations, or nature and explain how it is that the believer sees religious meaning in these things. But such teaching is necessarily one step removed from trying to get the pupil to experience the religiousness of them.

We have now looked at some of the main lines of approach in both the nature and function of religion in education. It is not being suggested that all RE teachers and writers on the subject fall into one or other of the categories described. Attitudes and approaches often blend. The philosopher's task in all this is to spotlight the meaning and implications of what is said in RE.

Summary of Chapter 4

Accurate and sympathetic observation and treatment of human experience are necessary aspects of good teaching practice. Religion as a curriculum subject, however, will continue to present problems of content, problems about what should or should not be included in the subject matter, so long as we ignore the ambiguities inherent in the phenomenological approach and in that of its foster-child 'implicit' RE.

Both in Wilson's thesis and in 'implicit' RE the question of whether the morality of a secular society has direct links with religion is at best opaque. It has been argued that these two fields of human experience should not be confused and that in any case religion cannot find its *raison d'être* within the precincts of human ethics.

We have argued, against Holley, that there is insufficient reason to think human beings have a spiritual dimension by nature and that all pupils are potentially religious. Further, we have tried to show that 'religious understanding' is reducible in an educational context to no more than an understanding of religion. We have concluded that there are no grounds for Holley's thesis that RE is 'central to all educational activities'.

Confessional or confessional-type approaches in RE are rejected as inappropriate to the teaching of religion in state schools. Yet confessionalism appears to persist in more covert ways. The manner in which 'choice' and 'truth' are handled in RE is also open to serious question.

*   *   *

5

Indoctrination, Commitment and Religious Education

'Indoctrination', like 'education', is a social concept. As such it may be thought about in many different ways. The fact that so much has been written on indoctrination within the philosophy of education at least alerts us to its possible significance in that field. That it is even more important for the RE teacher to be clear on the subject becomes evident as soon as the nature of religion in education is discussed in any depth. Unlike teachers of mathematics or geography, the teacher of religion, rather sooner than later, has to answer the accusation that he is, or is liable to be, 'indoctrinating'.

This raises the first question. How can it be so easily assumed, as it appears to be in the Western world, that indoctrination is in some way inherently bad or pejorative? To answer this we may consider some of the ways in which the term is used. It no longer appears to be the case that indoctrination is used only and always in the context of teaching doctrines. This, indeed, is the origin of the term, but there is nothing inherently wrong in the idea of 'teaching doctrines' for this phrase is itself only a more traditional way of describing instruction in areas of belief that may include science as well as politics and religion. Instruction concerning bodies of belief in our society is close to what may be traditionally thought of as 'education', and if we are not to waste time in endless speculation then finer conceptual analysis, perhaps the most important tool of the philosopher, will produce greater clarity. If therefore there is nothing noxious in its traditional use, what now makes 'indoctrination' pejorative, thus to be avoided, in education in general and RE in particular?

A snap answer to this may be found by considering comments made by a (hopefully) mythical tutor to a student teacher. How would the student react if, instead of saying 'You taught them well today', the tutor said 'You indoctrinated them well today'? Of course, the answer is not as simple as this, because the comments presuppose the nature of both 'taught' and 'indoctrination'. But the situation does illustrate the point that meaning and use have changed. If the student teacher makes a startled jump when confronted with the second comment then there is some hope for the teaching profession, for the student will want to know why his tutor thinks he has been indoctrinating pupils. If there is no reaction from the student, his tutor might suggest he become a politician instead. The first question that springs to mind is, why are people inclined to see the teaching of religion as a subject in which there is particularly likely to be an element of indoctrination? The broader question involved is, what are the elements of 'indoctrination' that make us wish to disown it in our teaching? We shall examine a number of statements about religion and indoctrination and from these pick out some elements of the concept of indoctrination that both philosophers and teachers of religion regard as characteristic and avoidable.

Professor Antony Flew writes (1972, p. 106):

> The most widespread and the most successful programme of indoctrination is that of the schools which maintain their separate and independent existence precisely in order to inculcate belief in the doctrines of the Roman Catholic Church. Any philosophy of education which is to be . . . adequately relevant and realistic has got to face this fact.

This is fighting talk and it needs to be qualified, but other philosophers have similar feelings about religious teaching.

> If schools attempt to initiate children into a particular religion, if, that is to say, they take particular steps with the intention of committing children to a set of beliefs, they are guilty of indoctrination. For we have defined indoctrination as the intentional implanting of belief so that it will stick, by non-rational means. (Barrow, 1981, p. 150)

Raymond Holley says (1978, pp. 19–20) that general aims in education:

> must be morally acceptable. It is in terms of this criterion that many opponents of religious education in county schools voice their most strident protests when they perceive such 'education' being used for purposes of 'conversion' or 'indoctrination' – and in this way they are right to make their protests . . . To treat a child as if he were necessarily and ineffably going to be a member of one's own *congregatio fidelium* is surreptitiously to deny the possibility of his deciding otherwise . . . to deny his potential autonomy.

What the teacher of religion has to do is decide as nearly as possible what the pitfalls are for him. And in order to determine that, he will need to consider those elements of indoctrination that have been picked out as detrimental to education. We can identify some four areas in the teaching situation where indoctrination in the pejorative sense may be used. These are: content, methods of teaching, the intention of the teacher and the aims of the teacher. Flew suggests that it is *content* that determines the nature of indoctrination, for indoctrination necessarily involves the inculcation of doctrine. Flew elaborates the argument that indoctrination necessarily involves the inculcation of specific kinds of doctrines as 'unshakeable beliefs' in cases where such beliefs are 'if not false, at least not by any ordinary standards known to be true'. He adds, 'if we do want to attend to whatever sorts of indoctrination are most common in Britain today, then it is very hard to find any serious rival to the religious for the first place' (Flew, 1972, p. 75).

James Gribble (1969), like Flew, places the emphasis in indoctrination on content. Indoctrination, he says, 'refers to the passing on of a body of beliefs which rest on assumptions which are either false or for which no publicly acceptable evidence is or can be provided.' Examples of this, he says, may be found in Marxism, Mormonism and Roman Catholicism. According to Gribble, doctrine is 'not a set of beliefs which are *publicly* testable, but rather the beliefs of a restricted number of people, the restriction being a necessary consequence of the inability of those who hold the beliefs to publicly demonstrate their truth'. Beliefs of this kind, Gribble asserts, may be contrasted with those of science and history, whose beliefs are publicly testable. The inculcation of isolated beliefs, true or false, are not cases of indoctrination, he says; they become so only when grouped into a set or body of beliefs.

John Wilson also picks out content as a distinguishing feature of indoctrination. He maintains: 'The model cases of indoctrination are obvious: brainwashing people to believe in Communism, teaching Christianity by the threat of torture or damnation, forcing people by early training to accept social roles as in Huxley's *Brave New World*' (Wilson, 1964, p. 26). Wilson asks: 'What is the difference between hypnotizing a boy to believe in Communism and hypnotizing him to master A Level physics? Plainly it is not a difference in *method*: it is rather a difference of subject-matter.' We would not object to hypnotic persuasion in mathematics or Latin grammar, says Wilson, whereas we would in political, religious and moral beliefs. The difference between these two groups of subjects, argues Wilson, lies in the nature of the subject. Whereas the contents of mathematics and Latin grammar can be presented as publicly accepted truths, the contents of politics, religion and morals cannot. Beliefs, of any kind, must be backed by 'publicly accepted evidence, not simply what sectarians like to consider as evidence' (p. 28). 'This principle [i.e. 'publicly accepted evidence'] consists in only educating children to adopt behaviour patterns and to have feelings which are seen by every sane and sensible person to be agreeable and necessary' (p. 34).

In pinpointing 'the intentional implanting of belief so that it will stick, by non-rational means' as a characterization of indoctrination, Robin Barrow shifts the emphasis from 'content' to *method* in the techniques used in teaching. Rejecting the idea that only 'doctrinal beliefs' can be indoctrinated' and the related view that 'only unprovable propositions themselves can be indoctrinated (i.e. ones that we do not know how to set about proving or disproving)', Barrow says: 'I know of no convincing argument for accepting either of these proposed limitations . . . I see nothing unintelligible, logically odd or peculiar in the idea of indoctrinating people with simple falsehoods or even truths' (1981, p. 52). The important element in considering whether something is indoctrination is the intention to get a belief (true or false) to stick by using non-rational means. The principle of rationality, for Barrow, can also determine the subject matter for indoctrination. 'Teaching people that four times four equals sixteen . . . can be explained and taught in a rational manner'; it is therefore not an example of indoctrination. On the other hand, 'teaching them that the theory of evolution is iniquitous and false' cannot be taught in a rational manner (it may be false but it can be rationally argued to be true), and is therefore an example of indoctrination. 'My definition of indoctrination, therefore, is: the use of non-rational means with the intention of implanting belief(s) unshakeably' (p. 53). The criterion 'intention' is not used with special weight in Barrow's argument, although it is there. We shall see in a moment what emphasis may be placed on 'intention' in indoctrination.

R. F. Atkinson, in his paper 'Instruction and indoctrination' (1965), also picks out method as a major characteristic of indoctrination. Where 'education' is seen to have the two elements, teaching 'that' (theories, propositions, etc.) and teaching 'how' (practical skills), says Atkinson, we may describe it as a process involving 'instruction' and 'training'. Both 'instruction' and 'training' involve the use of reason and understanding, the intelligence. The pair of words that may be opposed to these educational terms is 'indoctrination' (theories, etc.) and 'drilling' (practice, etc.). They stand in opposition because they do not require the use of intelligence and rationality. (Atkinson hastens to add: 'it seems inevitable that some recourse will sometimes be necessary to try to impart information and techniques beyond the recipients' understanding, that there will be some learning by rote or drill'; p. 173.) Since 'instruction is governed by criteria which are in principle accessible to any rational person' it is 'a matter of treating a person as an end in himself', and this is morally unacceptable. On the other hand, 'indoctrination' exploits a person as a means to further ends, and this is morally unacceptable.

Barrow has involved the notion of 'intention' within the concept of indoctrination: schools which have the 'intention of committing children to a set of [particularly religious] beliefs . . . are guilty of indoctrination.'

John White raised the *intention* element to the point where it becomes a single, necessary and sufficient, criterion for distinguishing indoctrination. ' "Indoctrination" . . . is definable solely in terms of intention' (White, 1967, p. 181). White defines it like this: 'Indoctrinating someone is trying to get him to believe that a proposition "p" is true, in such a way that nothing will shake that belief.' He therefore denies that subject matter (religious beliefs, political ideologies, etc.) is characteristic of the concept, and also that any specific method marks out a process of indoctrination. Quite apart from unintended indoctrination, which White thinks logically possible (for example, the effects of an implicit acceptance of the existence of God in discussion), there is 'reason to be concerned about the possibility of indoctrination in religion . . . in the full-blooded intentional sense' (p. 189). White therefore places emphasis on the 'task' function of 'indoctrination' (which, like 'education', has both 'task' and 'achievement' senses). 'The difficulty with religious education', he goes on, 'is that if the teacher denies having this intention, it is hard to see what other intention he might have which is compatible with there being such a subject as religious education' (p. 190). This is because if a teacher in the classroom goes beyond the debate on fundamental questions such as the existence of God or immortality it will have to be assumed that the class is 'rationally convinced of the truth of the basic propositions'. And 'if rational conviction is here impossible, it is difficult to see how one could teach religion (*qua* religion) without indoctrinating'. If, on the other hand, the teacher claims to be teaching merely 'historically about the life of Jesus or the Prophets', White argues, then there is 'the doubt whether, while he is certainly teaching history, he is still teaching religion'.

Atkinson drew our attention to the moral aspect among the dangers of indoctrination by invoking the Kantian principle that morality dictates that people should be treated as ends rather than means. The indoctrinator abuses this moral principle by 'exploiting' people, by using them as means, thereby diminishing their powers of responsibility as individuals. This view is highlighted by the quotation taken from Holley. 'Children are potential persons', argues Holley, 'and a person is an autonomous being' (1978, p. 20). In this sense Holley offers a case against indoctrination in terms of *moral aims*. 'The moral propriety of educational activity', he argues, 'resides in the contribution which it makes to personal autonomy.' Being 'autonomous', he says, is part of the concept 'person'. To take away the possibility of a child's becoming autonomous 'by dint of influence' and so on 'is immoral'. Holley has a further point to make. He turns the problem of indoctrination against the anti-RE lobby. The fear of indoctrination that could lead, as some might hope, to the abolition of RE in schools, would have an adverse effect on education as a whole. 'To label religious education unfairly as "indoctrination", and thereby to campaign for its removal from an educational curriculum, is to embrace a form of socialization which is itself indoctrinatory. And that is morally irresponsible'.

These are some of the areas of thought on indoctrination that might concern the teacher of religion. There is a case for considering the subject seriously because the signs are that there remain many in society – religious groups as well as humanists and others – who still regard much of what goes on in RE as one form or another of indoctrination. The signs are, too, that they may be right. Only the RE teacher who is prepared to face the questions involved in the concept of indoctrination will be armed with appropriate responses. The first step will be for the teacher to acquaint himself with what others have said on the subject. This we have begun. The second step is to probe, to question more closely, arguments and conclusions that at first sight seem convincing. This, too, has already been begun in the literature. For example, in the volume edited by Snook we find Wilson countering some of the points made by Flew, and Flew, in turn replying to Wilson. Barrow (1981) implicitly criticizes Flew when Barrow argues against 'those who maintain that only doctrinal beliefs can be indoctrinated'. White (1967) declares Atkinson's analysis (1965) to be inadequate. And so on.

The third step is to try to apply our thinking on the matter to the very practical job of teaching religion. Whatever theoretical interests we may have or discover in considering the problem of indoctrination, at the end of the day it is our classroom practice that must benefit. There is a danger to be recognized if we think it a simple matter to ask questions arising from the immediate classroom situation. For example, do we teach the Christian doctrine of the Trinity as an 'unshakeable belief'? If we do, does our teaching fall into Flew's or White's category of indoctrination? When teaching the parable of the Prodigal Son do we too readily assume that religious concepts like 'sin', 'reconciliation' and 'mercy' are established 'facts' that all pupils already know and accept? If we do, are we, intentionally or unintentionally, getting pupils unquestioningly to accept such dogmas by default? The danger is that if the pejorative interpretation of indoctrination is accepted then no one is going to admit that he is indoctrinating. Now, the interesting thing about this negative response is that we should probably deny the charge of indoctrination *whatever* characteristic is being looked at, whether it be content, method, intention, moral aim, or any combination of these. But does our denial really mean that we are never likely to indoctrinate any pupil at any time – it's always the other fellow? Dr Obispo, in Huxley's novel *After Many a Summer*, says 'Iagos don't exist. People will do everything Iago did; but they'll never say they're villains.' The observation should act as a caution, reminding us of White's claim that indoctrination may go on unintentionally, and of Barrow's claim that a teacher can also indoctrinate pupils with 'simple truths'.

While we must certainly bring our considered judgements to bear on the classroom situation, then, there is no substitute for first probing the meaning of the concept itself and the ways in which it has so far been characterized. This is not the place for a full-scale critique of the views so briefly presented. I wish only to point out ways in which we may begin to clarify our own understanding of the matter; for 'indoctrination' is not just a playground for academic philosophers. It is a problem that can be pursued for the purpose of improving the status, teaching techniques and content of RE in schools.

We can start by questioning Flew's idea that indoctrination means the inculcating of doctrines as unshakeable beliefs, by pointing out that the ideas 'inculcating' and 'unshakeable' are unclear. 'To inculcate' may mean no more than 'to impress upon', a task to which no teacher is a stranger. Does 'unshakeable' refer to a period of time? Of both Flew's and White's notion 'unshakeable' we may ask, if a person is a devout Roman Catholic up to the age of 25, but rejects the church's teaching after that age, can we say he was indoctrinated? Must the effects of indoctrination last a lifetime, or less? If less, for how long? Edward Hulmes makes a comment it is appropriate to remember here: 'Some of the most consistently vociferous opponents of the indoctrinatory aspect of religious education were apparently subjected to its rigours in their school days. Their escape from its consequences is all the more remarkable' (Hulmes, 1979, p. 13). But perhaps the main objection to Flew's main point – that of inculcating *doctrine* – is that the concept of 'indoctrination' is not generally used only to describe 'doctrine' and the way it is taught in church or state schools, as Flew asserts that it is; its uses are far wider. This being so, we cannot characterize indoctrination in the extremely narrow terms of either 'doctrine' or the way that doctrine is taught. Flew's further objection, namely, that doctrines taught in the way he describes are 'if not false, at least not by any ordinary standards known to be true', begs the question of how we can determine statements of 'truth' in religion. It is not at all certain that verification of beliefs – of any sort – can be accepted by empirical means alone. We have seen that there are other ways by which we might arrive at true statements.

Wilson claims that 'the concept of indoctrination concerns the truth and evidence of beliefs', therefore 'the beliefs we teach must be rational.' He says 'Religious, political and moral beliefs are *uncertain*' and must be objected to as indoctrinatory, while subjects like mathematics and Latin grammar are certain and cannot be subjects of indoctrination. One might well imagine teachers of art, music, literature and history asking Wilson in what way their subjects could be pronounced *certain* (for even historians would not think of their subject matter as a collection of so many 'certain' facts). The right to be certain holds many problems for the epistemologist and it is perhaps a little naïve to make bold statements of this nature. And if by 'uncertain' Wilson means 'not capable of verification', then again we have to point out that there are different ways of verifying something, and perhaps no statement can ever be 'certain'. No less a person than Einstein had the same doubt. In his lecture to the Prussian Academy of Sciences in 1921 Einstein said: 'as far as the propositions of mathematics refer to reality, they are not certain; and as far as they are certain, they do not refer to reality'.

Barrow asserts, as we have seen, that whatever can be taught in a rational manner cannot be called indoctrination. Contrariwise, 'the use of non-rational means with the intention of implanting belief(s) unshakeably' is indoctrination. We have looked at difficulties arising from the idea of 'unshakeability'. One might argue that this emphasis on 'rationality' is the weakest of all characteristics so far considered. There is the inherent difficulty of determining precisely what rational methods would, without question, rule out a specific case of indoctrination. Is it being claimed that all hardline communists, racists and committed religious believers have necessarily been indoctrinated? If they have not been indoctrinated then they must have become committed to their beliefs by rational means. One feels that Barrow would not wish to accept this conclusion. Yet surely it can be claimed that at least some committed Muslims, communists and Roman Catholics have good reasons for their beliefs; they are able to argue eminently reasonably for their views in much the same way as those who hold certain political views on utilitarianism. Arthur Koestler in *Darkness at Noon* is able to show just how rational and logical indoctrinated communists can be. Referring to the principles of the communist revolution, the character Rubshov says:

> 'We have thrown overboard all conventions, our sole guiding principle is that of the consequent logica; we are sailing without ethical ballast.' Perhaps the heart of the evil lay there. Perhaps it did not suit mankind to sail without ballast. And perhaps reason alone was a defective compass.

We may say that implanting beliefs non-rationally can be one reason for thinking that a teacher who practises such methods may be indoctrinating his pupils, but it is neither a necessary nor a sufficient condition for asserting that indoctrination is going on without further discussion. The criterion of 'rationality' therefore is not, by itself, a characterization of 'indoctrination' that carries conviction.

In confining indoctrination to the intention of the teacher to get pupils 'to believe that a proposition "p" is true, in such a way that nothing will shake that belief', White rather strictly limits the ways in which we actually use the word. For instance, it has been said that 'indoctrination' is both a 'task' and an 'achievement' word; we can *try* to indoctrinate and we can *succeed* in indoctrinating. We may, however, try to indoctrinate without succeeding; similarly we may succeed without trying. This is how we use the word. In stressing the teacher's 'intention' to get pupils to believe something unshakeably, White offers a criterion for only the 'task' sense of the concept; the teacher *intends* to teach in a certain way. But we feel we want to be able to say that even where a teacher has the intention of teaching in the way described he may not in fact be indoctrinating, for he is not succeeding. And is it not possible that where a teacher does not have the intention of teaching in the way described, he may still succeed in getting a pupil to believe a 'proposition "p" is true, in such a way that nothing will shake that belief'?

Holley's case against indoctrination rests on the claim that it denies the moral aim of education which is to develop the pupil's 'potential autonomy'. The argument is similar to Atkinson's objection to indoctrination on the grounds that it exploits a person rather than 'treating a person as an end in himself'. What force is there in this criticism? It would appear quite possible for teachers to put first objectives that disregard the pupil as an end in himself. We can imagine this happening in totalitarian states where the interests of the individual are subjugated to those of the state. Such an objective is explicit in Plato's educational plan for the Guardians of his ideal state. The education of the Guardian is aimed at the good of the state *by means of* the individual. Music, poetry, and literature among other things, are to be strictly censored before being taught to pupil Guardians. A similar attitude can be detected in one part of Hegel's thinking, thence into modern totalitarian states of both left and right. For Hegel 'the state is not merely an institution invented for the settling of conflicts or the organization of collective enterprises in accordance with a social contract . . . it is the realization of freedom, an end in itself . . . the reality which alone gives value to the individual life' (Kolakowski, 1978, Vol. 1, p. 73). (The state, for Hegel, is not, of course, an expression of the 'will of the majority', but the will of the historical Reason.)

Now it is very easy for us in parliamentary Britain to think that restrictions placed on individuals for the 'good' of the state or for other ideals like those of Christianity or Islam are restrictions on autonomy and therefore a meaningful interpretation of 'indoctrination'. But the notion of autonomy implies a measure of self-government and nothing in the logic of Marxism, Islam, or Christianity necessarily denies this. In our own multi-cultural society, restrictions, legal barriers and different kinds of censorship are woven into the pattern of the community and of education, but we do not normally protest that they deny our autonomy. Instead we give them names like 'law and order' and teach pupils to observe the 'rules' of society knowing that they are not necessarily a denial of our autonomy. We often teach our children to put the 'good' of the majority above the 'good' of the individual. And we do not allow them to choose their own curriculum. Teachers, universities and society in general determine what shall be taught. Teachers can always claim to have the pupil's interests at heart, even when they cannot know for sure what those interests are, for teachers are themselves products of the system. But *if* such attitudes are forms of indoctrination we do not claim, without further discussion, that they therefore deny autonomy to the individual. In short, it is not at all easy to determine where, in the delicate tensions of a liberal democracy, to draw the line between treating individuals as ends and treating them as means; or that the line, if drawn, will clearly distinguish between a 'good' and a 'bad' state of affairs. If we can assume, then, that indoctrination restricts the development of 'potential autonomy', we cannot say that this is necessarily morally objectionable.

It should be emphasized that neither the views of indoctrination presented here nor the lines of questioning I have taken are comprehensive. The important thing is that teachers of RE should be aware of some of the current problems discussed concerning the concept of indoctrination and its connections with religion. And after considering what has been said about indoctrination, and after probing the concept further, we may at least become sensitive to the possibility that RE is a prime area for indoctrination.

The idea that a pupil might become 'committed' to some form of religious belief through the teaching of RE in state schools is, in a word, anathema to many unbelievers. It is this, together with the implication that rational thought processes have been avoided, that often raises the fear of indoctrination in religious education. But is 'commitment' the bogy it is made out to be? For one thing, we cannot just assume that to be committed is to be non-rational in certain important respects.

Consider, first, the argument of Edward Hulmes. What makes Hulmes able to assert 'Commitment is both the point of departure and the final goal of all religious education' (Hulmes, 1979, p. 87)? It can be asked, says Hulmes, whether teachers who claim to be more objective and neutral are any less committed to certain beliefs and actions than teachers with clearly marked religious commitments.

> Unless a teacher is bereft of ideas and imagination, he has a basic commitment which influences the way in which he works . . . Such a commitment may be no more acceptable in teaching than an identifiably *religious* commitment, and potentially more tendentious precisely because it purports to be 'neutral'. (ibid., p. 21; original italics)

Hulmes goes on: 'The case against the committed teacher is incomplete unless other kinds of commitment [for example, the agnostic or secularist] are recognized for what they are' (p. 21). In distinguishing between 'religious education' and 'religious studies' Hulmes argues that 'religious education is concerned with something wider' (p. 31). And when children ask ' "But which religion is right?" ' . . . they are surely entitled to help in

70

discriminating between the options presented to them' (pp. 31–2). To aid children in this choice is an educational issue connected to 'the pupil's *own* experience and needs' (p. 31; Hulmes's italics throughout) while 'religious studies', it may be assumed, are not necessarily so connected. Mere description of religion 'along strictly phenomenological lines will tend to eliminate the immediacy of religious experience . . . It is pretentious to speak about the teacher as one who communicates insights when the emphasis in religious education is on a *description* of what the adherents of different religions believe and do. The word "insights" here seems curiously inappropriate for an educational activity designed to collect data' (p. 31). Children need help in '*decision-making*' (p. 33). Hulmes cites with approval the comments of Jerome Brunner ' "Somebody who does not see anything beautiful and powerful about mathematics is not likely to ignite others with a sense of the intrinsic excitement of the subject" ' and adds 'what is true of the teacher of mathematics is true, *a fortiori*, of the teacher of religious education' (p. 37).

Moreover, claims Hulmes, the attempt to adopt a 'degree of studied neutrality' in RE misses an essential ingredient. 'The essence of religion – the commitment and potential for worshipping response in the individual – is excluded. Religious *education* is cut off from its source of life and power' (p. 50). 'It is the essence of religion', says Hulmes, 'that it changes lives' (p. 49). 'Religious education is defective if children are obliged to learn *about* Islam instead of being helped to measure up to the difference that Islam would make to their lives. What is true in respect to Islam, is true also of Christianity and of every other alternative religious option' (p. 52). 'Commitment is not merely *one* of the aspects of religion. It is, ultimately, what religion is about' (p. 79).

Religious education, for Hulmes, involves helping pupils to make decisions about religion, for it is in the nature of religion to demand acceptance or rejection, and the committed religious teacher who has an 'obligation to declare his commitment' is best able to do this (p. 33). Hulmes's position is not simply a retreat to traditional 'confessionalism'. 'The purpose of religious education is [not] to compel the individual to accept a particular form of institutionalized religious belief' (p. 99). RE 'has nothing to do with "evangelizing" or "proselytizing" ' and '*preaching* is not a valid form of teaching in schools' (p. 90). It is likely that many educationists would remain unconvinced. If Hulmes's presentation of RE is not a strong form of evangelizing, a form of indoctrination and a call to blind commitment, they might respond, then what could be? It is true that Hulmes's argument lacks philosophical force in that, for example, he does not put forward an unmistakable case in support of the assertion 'indoctrination is next to impossible'. Perhaps, for indoctrination, he does not see the need for such an argument; it is sufficient (as well as necessary) to hold that, given the appropriate insights into religion, 'the children will ultimately have to choose for themselves' (p. 90). For 'the controversial nature of religion does not make it an exception [among school subjects] provided that free and critical engagement is guaranteed to the child in considering the evidence. This is the only safeguard against indoctrination in any subject' (p. 101). Such comments can only serve to deny that Hulmes advocates what might be called 'blind commitment', for talk of 'free and critical engagement' can surely not contribute to intellectual blindness.

For Hulmes, 'commitment' is not a problem in RE: it is a solution to the meaning of religion. For the pupil 'commitment' is 'the seeking, the questioning, the finding, the revising' by means of which the 'data' of religion may be understood (p. 87). Pupils, like teachers, are committed to 'seeking', to 'finding' and to 'revising' what can be known of religion. For the teacher 'the ideal form of commitment, interpreted as an essential tool in [his hands] — would be a commitment which is firm, but provisional, or partial . . . in that the search may discover fresh evidence in the light of which the commitment is to be modified' (p. 88). It is possible that critics of commitment in RE are objecting to committing children to an extreme subjective 'faith'. But Hulmes advances the important point that it is necessary 'to preserve the distinction between faith and knowledge' (p. 88).

Roger Trigg draws our attention to the thesis that 'all commitments must involve beliefs which may turn out to be true or false' (Trigg, 1973, p. 43) and that 'the importance of the propositional element in any commitment cannot be over-emphasised' (p. 46). Trigg is able to criticize both Wittgenstein and Tillich precisely on the grounds that they are 'preoccupied with the element of commitment in faith' and ignore 'the element of propositional belief' (pp. 57–8). 'The belief provides a reason for commitment', Trigg argues, 'but is logically separate from it. The belief could occur without commitment, even where what is believed in is the Resurrection' (p. 79). In maintaining the distinction between faith and knowledge and, as it would appear, in maintaining the need for pupils and teachers alike to come to understand fully the propositions of religious knowledge as a basis for commitment, Hulmes is also maintaining the possibility for objective, open choice. An open choice *means* conceding the possibility that the pupil will reject religious commitment, for 'commitment is inextricably bound up with choice' (Hulmes, 1979, p. 82).

Nevertheless, it is at this point, perhaps, that the structure of Hulmes's argument is seen to lack consistency and conviction; for where the logic of open choice leads to a pupil's rational rejection of a religious commitment Hulmes refuses to follow. Hulmes's thinking on open choice appears to go only as far as recognizing that 'the finding of truth by the individual is an integral part of the searching process' (pp. 43–4) and thereby collapsing the conceptual distinction that may surely be made between 'searching' and 'finding'. Such a refusal undermines much of the force of Hulmes's desire to help pupils sort out their own 'experience and needs' and reduces commitment as 'the final goal of all religious education' to, at most, a commitment to find out which religion is the 'right' one, or, perhaps, to find out what religion is 'about' – a mere shadow of what Hulmes intended.

Hulmes does not reject the use of reason in the forming of religious commitment. 'Adherents of different religions . . . would not wish to deny the fundamental educational point that information presented *about* their various faiths requires to be evaluated in some way so as to distinguish between what is demonstrably reasonable and what is clearly unreasonable.' However, Hulmes continues, 'On the other hand insistence on the primacy of reason in religious education creates difficulties of its own. The paragon of reason may turn out to be an emotional machine, incapable of understanding the first thing about religious experience, or the claims that religion makes on him.' Hulmes asks, 'Is it not a questionable assumption in religious education that the phenomena of religion reveal their meaning to *rational* scrutiny?' (p. 41). The logical tangle exposed in these remarks – for example, that we must distinguish between the reasonable and the unreasonable but that it is doubtful whether this can be done by rational means – brings into serious question Hulmes's idea of 'education'. Can it be that Hulmes is suggesting that boundaries should be put to intellectual inquiry in education? Are we to accept, without question, certain mystical or inexplicable forms of religious experience and knowledge? For Hulmes declares: 'It is not given to us, as teachers of religious education . . . to *explain* the mystery of that love of [God in Christ]' (pp. 102–3). Are we to teach certain propositional elements in religious belief, for example, that God is one in three and three in one, without also teaching truth criteria for such propositions?

What would Hulmes put in place of the questioning attitude in education? It is, perhaps, no accident that Hulmes places emphasis on 'explanation' and on 'clarification' of religion rather than on an open-ended inquiry into religious propositions for he tends, in the end, to minimize the role of reason in religion. The influence of reason in Western culture, he says, dominates our thinking concerning religion.

> One consequence of this continuing culture-bound domination is the subordination of faith to reason, and the elimination of that which is found in faith but held to be contrary to reason . . . The use of reason can help to clarify *why* certain features of religion are obscure, but that is the limit of its function (pp. 77–8; original italics)

It would appear that, despite disclaimers, Hulmes must stop rational discourse in RE at some point, even though he allows that a pupil might become committed by rational procedures. It is true that we cannot, ultimately, deny to pupils commitment to religious, political, or moral beliefs. What the committed teacher can do is distinguish quite clearly between his own enthusiasm for a subject and attempts to persuade pupils into one way of life rather than another. The former is a professional teaching virtue while the latter is arguably anti-educational.

Some argue that RE is a different kind of subject from others on the curriculum. Peter Gardner (1980, p. 163) considers that 'religion is a special case'. Comparing religion with aesthetics Gardner says (p. 164):

> an individual's aesthetic beliefs do not determine his life in the way that a theist's religious beliefs determine his. In this respect it can be claimed that we should be much more careful about how we teach religion than how we teach aesthetics.

Unless the underpinning criteria of an educational process lie in a strictly utilitarian or instrumental context it is hard to see why we should be more careful in our teaching of one subject than in another. If we were teaching pupils to be religious, or if we were teaching normative values in moral education, there might be something in the argument, for then we should be more pointedly determining a pupil's life. Since, however, we teach religion 'because it is there' (to follow Hulmes's wording), because we want pupils to understand the world; and since we teach aesthetics, history and science for the same reason and do not, as educationists, persuade pupils to become painters, historians and scientists but even provide them with rational abilities to disagree with us – Gardner's argument is without logical point. On the practical level it seems to me that much of the problematic nature of RE comes from regarding it as a special case. Teachers able and willing to teach all other subjects to their primary school classes will draw the line at RE; mathematics or English specialists in secondary schools asked to help out in another subject will express either strong aversion to or marked enthusiasm for RE as an alternative. If education is to be seen as bringing young people to the threshold of adult activities, to the point where they are able to dispense with their teacher, to the point – but not beyond it – where mature decisions have to be made, then there seems to be no educational reason for treating RE as a special case. Arguments brought forward to maintain its special status would seem to be more relevant to religion than to religious education. And this would apply with equal force to comments made by Dearden, cited in Gardner's article (ibid., note 41, p. 168), to the effect that while we do not doubt that, in aesthetics, beautiful things exist, we do doubt the existence of God. On these grounds a special status can be given to religion, says Dearden. But this is to confuse religion with RE. In the process of debating the existence of God in the classroom we are involved with religious education and this is not in itself, of course, a question of doubt or disquiet. Furthermore, education is as much concerned with what people think is true as with what they think they know, and the problem is not peculiar to RE. It is certainly not new to philosophy to be unable to distinguish between the two positions. And is beauty *not* in the eye of the beholder?

Grimmitt contends that commitment arises as a problem when RE is confused with 'religious nurture'. RE is, for Grimmitt, a combination of the phenomenological approach that 'enables those features of religion which constitute its distinctiveness as a study or discipline to be identified or elucidated' with that aspect which will enable the pupil to '*learn from* religion about himself' (Grimmitt, 1981, pp. 48–9; original italics throughout). These two elements comprise what Grimmitt calls 'the process of religious education'. RE, in this sense, is wider than the view that religious education is to be equated with 'religious studies'. Commitment, Grimmitt goes on, is a feature of all three approaches – religious nurture, religious studies and religious education. The activities and intentions of the 'religious nurturer' are directed towards bringing about religious commitment in the pupil similar to the teacher's own commitment. On the other hand, Grimmitt's 'process of education' incorporating the activities of the 'religious educator' and the phenomenological, objective features of 'religious studies' 'specifically allows for pupils to be offered an "education in commitment", i.e. an understanding of what "commitment" or "making a faith commitment" involves and an awareness of the way in which their own identities are shaped by the commitments they have made and will make' (p. 51).

There is a 'considerable gulf', says Grimmitt, between religious nurture and religious education. It is a dangerous 'over-simplification' to think that the difference between them is merely that 'the religious nurturer is free to press for a religious commitment while the religious educator is not' or that 'the religious nurturer can be "confessional" in his presentation of content while the religious educator can not' (p. 46). More fundamentally, 'the religious educator is essentially a "secular educator concerned with the study of religion" ' (p. 43). While the 'religious adherent' presents his own religion as 'Truth', and 'other truths are judged by this Truth . . . the object of study', the 'religious educator' is concerned with 'religion's *educational* worth . . . at variance with' the view of the 'religious nurturer' who is, by definition, concerned with nurturing a specific religious commitment (loc.cit.).

Grimmitt's article is intended to provide us with a new view of RE. (Grimmitt presents a shorter version of the same view in 'World religions and personal development', Grimmitt, 1982, ch. 12.) This is the view that 'R.E.'s prime responsibility and function is not to produce phenomenologists of religion but to help pupils to come to terms with questions about their own identity, their own values and life-styles, their own priorities and commitments, and their own frame of reference for viewing life and giving it meaning' (Grimmitt, 1981, p. 49). The study of religion 'from an educational point of view' is concerned with 'meaning-making and truth-making . . . to promote critical consciousness, self-knowledge and self-awareness; to develop skills necessary for the interpretation of personal, social, moral and religious issues and experiences; to extend capacities for personal decision-making'. With these insights and skills the pupil will not only *'learn about'* religion but also learn *'from religion* about himself'. It is Grimmitt's contention that equipped with such personal insights the pupils will be able to understand what 'making a faith commitment' means and the meaning of commitments they have made or will make themselves.

This form of commitment — to an understanding of religious commitment in others and in pupils themselves — is, for Grimmitt, distinctively educational and therefore quite different from the religious commitment aimed at by the 'religious nurturer'. The precise difference appears to be that while the religious educator teaches with the objective that pupils shall understand commitment, the 'religious nurturer' teaches 'from faith and is directed towards faith'. However, the difference between the two forms of commitment is not as strong as Grimmitt makes out. It would appear quite possible for the RE teacher who wishes to bring about religious commitment in his pupils to also bring about in them an understanding of commitment in others as well as a better appreciation of their own commitment. Hulmes, for example, would advocate a similar position (cf. Hulmes, 1979, pp. 100 and *passim*). Again, as we have seen, a teacher who aims at bringing about religious commitment in his pupils does not necessarily have to avoid the educational principles emphasized by Grimmitt (1981, p. 43):

> Such principles [of the secular educator] relate to the manner in which subject disciplines, including religion, should be investigated — in a manner which assists the development of 'cognitive perspective' or rationality, promotes understanding of the structure and procedures of the disciplines, recognizes the integrity, autonomy and voluntariness of the pupil.

Both the 'religious educator' and the 'religious nurturer' can agree on these principles and if there is a problem of commitment between the 'educator' and 'nurturer' it is to be found elsewhere.

The new element in RE advocated by Grimmitt — that the pupil should learn *'from* religion about himself'* — might prove to be a source of confusion for the teacher. No doubt most would agree that Grimmitt's description of 'the process of religious education' – helping pupils to come to terms with 'their own identity', helping them to sort out the meaning of life, developing self-awareness, and so on – contains genuine educational goals. But unless we are to suppose that these goals are directly connected to the promotion of some form of commitment, religious or agnostic (both of which Grimmitt seems to reject), we must conclude that such recommendations are the goals of education in general, for there seems to be nothing especially 'religious' about them. Literature, history, science and music are all concerned with the development of 'meaning', 'identity', 'critical consciousness', and so on, in the pupil. RE is not alone in trying to promote the pupil's 'search for meaning and his involvement in meaning-making and truth-making' (whatever *that* means). Such ambiguous generalities, like the notorious 'education is for the whole man', tell us nothing more about the specific contribution of RE to education nor do they tell us what it is in RE that will enable the pupil to '*learn from* religion about himself'. But they do lead one to suspect that Grimmitt is reaching for some sort of personal commitment to life that is 'religious' in all but name; for the terms he uses here are reminiscent of the confessional-type language used in *What Can I Do in RE?* (1973). Grimmitt wrote there: 'Although the learning of facts and the development of concepts are integral to much of R.E., by far the most important area in R.E. is that concerned with promoting attitudes and values' (p. 131). One may wonder if such an approach is substantially different from the avowedly committed religious, or 'religious nurture', approach of Edward Hulmes. Of moral values (which he would also include in RE) Grimmitt states, with the implication that it should be approved, that there is 'more than a grain of truth' in 'the adage that morals or values are "caught rather than taught" ' (ibid., p. 78). Is it a viable aim of education, one might ask, to instil or promote certain distinctive personal attitudes while implicitly rejecting others? And Grimmitt is not unaware of this criticism. 'To speak, then, of the aims of moral education', he says, 'in terms of "inculcating favourable attitudes to . . . " is to invite both criticism and censure although in actual fact little headway is likely to be made in helping pupils to translate their moral judgments into moral patterns of conduct if such an aim is avoided.'

The emphasis Grimmitt places on efforts to get pupils to change their behavioural patterns and to translate their knowledge of religion into 'personal terms' cannot escape the suggestion that he wishes to throw out overt attempts at religious commitment through the front door and leave the back door open for more covert forms of religious commitment, despite the disclaimer 'we must avoid pressing pupils to commit themselves to find answers' (1982, p. 141). Perhaps it would serve RE better, in schools where inquiry rather than commitment is encouraged, if teachers taught pupils to question, and even to doubt, before calling on them to presuppose that they have a 'personal religious or spiritual dimension' to develop (1982, p. 143). Any teaching activity, whether in morals or religion, that attempts to 'inculcate', 'induce', 'implant', or 'promote' one particular set of social attitudes or one particular group of religious beliefs will remain open to the charge of indoctrination or the real possibility of premature and non-educational commitment.

Summary of Chapter 5

The possibility of indoctrination in RE, in the pejorative sense of the term, is considered by many to be one of the dangers in teaching religion in state schools. We have briefly examined ways by which indoctrination may be characterized. These are in terms of: (1) content, specifically doctrines, (2) method, involving teaching by non-rational means, (3) intention, as when a teacher intends to teach unshakeable religious or political belief, and (4) the morally objectionable characteristic that would deny the development of autonomy in pupils. We have seen that no single interpretation is entirely satisfactory and that it will remain possible for a teacher always to deny that he is indoctrinating. If, however, we accept that indoctrination can be characterized by one or more of these unwanted elements (and certainly the word is *used* to describe some form of undesirable teaching), then the danger can be lessened or avoided altogether by some analysis of the kind that has been discussed.

As with indoctrination, the idea that religious commitment might be connected in one way or another to RE is a reason for disquiet for many people. Theorists are generally agreed that preaching or evangelizing – which often leads to religious commitment – is not acceptable as part of a public process of education and that, instead, there should be open, rational inquiry. We have seen, however, that rational inquiry, if its emphasis is on explanation and clarification of religious ideas and stops short of the possibility of the rejection of religion, does not necessarily mean that teachers will avoid or even try to avoid bringing about religious commitment in pupils. We have argued that a religiously committed teacher can and should distinguish between enthusiasm for his own beliefs on the one hand and, on the other, his natural desire to bring pupils to a religious commitment.

We have seen that some theorists tend to collapse the distinction between 'searching' and 'finding' and to suppose that a 'search' necessarily means there is something − an 'identity'?, a 'spiritual dimension'? − to be found. It is not appropriate, we conclude, to teach in a way that presupposes that some form of religious commitment will or ought eventually to be made.

*   *   *

6

Teaching Religion

Two distinctive but interrelated characteristics can be discerned emerging from theories and practice in contemporary RE. There is, first, the changing nature of its content. Then there is a 'practical' element that seeks to involve pupils in what could be called 'first order' activities. It is important to look at these developments within a framework of education where 'study' is a central and determining feature. The main components of the new content have already been briefly discussed. These appear to be (i) religions other than Christianity, (ii) ethics (sometimes under the heading of moral education), and (iii) life-stances and non-religious world views. Broadening the scope of RE to include a study of other religions hardly calls for comment for it is a natural development of a religious teaching which no longer takes the view that RE is an arm of the proselytizing Christian church. The position is different with regard to (ii) and (iii).

We have seen that a special emphasis on morality might be counter-productive for both religion and ethics since it cannot be assumed that a religious code of behaviour can be equated with modern secular morality, nor that the morality of a secular world can be reduced to an aspect of religion. Colin Alves writes: 'If society wants moral education, then let it call for moral education, and not pervert the nature of another (even if allied) subject in order to achieve its purposes' (Alves, 1975, p. 26).

The study of life-stances and non-religious world views within RE poses, as we have seen, further and more complicated issues of demarcation. It is not being suggested that communism, trade unions, or the plight of the Third World, and so on, are not important areas for study within education. But it is at this point that the problem arises. It is questionable, to say the least, whether the world, with its great variety of traditions and problems, is specifically or even closely to be connected to RE. Such areas of study are better seen, it is suggested, as the subject matter for education. The problem for the RE teacher is, what can be reasonably regarded as the lines of demarcation for religion *within* education? It is reasonable for the RE teacher to suppose,

80

with W. D. Hudson, that his subject matter can be limited to the well-marked boundaries traditionally focused on the idea of 'god' (Hudson, 1973, p. 190). And this approach is not dictated by a reactionary point of view but by the nature of religion as it is generally understood by religious people. Such a demarcation of the subject also has the support of Hirst's 'forms of knowledge' theory, discussed and elaborated in Chapter 2, which, despite weaknesses, offers a more rational basis than some RE theorists who advocate a 'world view' approach. (Ninian Smart's article 'Why the West needs to see the world as others see it' in the *Times Higher Education Supplement*, 1 January 1982, is an illuminating example – with its eye-catching phrase 'cross-cultural worldview analysis' – of how theorists sometimes confuse what is possibly wrong with our educational system *as a whole* with what is to be taught within different areas of the curriculum.) 'Why', asks Hudson, 'call all this "religious education"?' (loc. cit.).

So much for developments in the content of RE. What, now, is to be said of the element of personal involvement in RE? It should be said at once that pupil involvement is not so much a new element as a new direction of involvement, for there is nothing new in teachers' attempts to initiate pupils into leading a Christian (Muslim, Jewish, etc.) way of life. Clearly, as Cox (1983, p. 143) points out, getting children to behave in one way rather than another has something to do with the content of what is taught in RE. Those who advocate the implicit religious approach not only propose that RE may be involved in an integrated studies programme but also strongly imply that RE is the curriculum subject *par excellence*, able to offer guidance in a pupil's personal life. Thus Cox suggests that RE helps us 'to decide how to make ourselves useful' and 'how to treat others' (p. 138). Grimmitt, treading a careful path between a purely academic phenomenological approach and that of the 'religious nurturer', says that the religious educator 'seeks to devise learning-situations which are sufficiently engaging at a personal level to stimulate each pupil to become involved in a form of "interior dialogue" ' about themselves in which a search for 'what or who I am' is of the utmost significance (Grimmitt, 1981, p. 50). The RE teacher, sensitive to the educational demands of his profession, may ask whether such commitment-forming attitudes do not go too far. Most contemporary RE teachers and writers have taken to heart, rightly so, Whitehead's observation that the 'merely well-informed man is the most useless bore on God's earth', together with Smart's view that 'education and learning transcend the informative'. But if RE, like other subjects, is seen to be more than an information-giving process, this does not necessarily mean that it must get pupils actively to engage in, for example, 'being useful', or that RE has the specific task of helping pupils to 'come to terms with questions about their own identity'. Surely, a teacher might reasonably suggest, whether a pupil is going to be 'useful' in society or whether he is to find his own 'identity' is a problem for education *as a whole*. A teacher of history or geography or mathematics does not normally demand a specifically historical, geographical, or mathematical orientation to the life of a pupil, *qua* pupil. The cry of over-intellectualism in RE no doubt expresses a desire to make the subject more personally interesting to the pupil, but that is largely a problem of teaching methods and cannot seriously affect the nature of the educational enterprise. For RE, like other subjects, is characteristically a process of *study*; a process which, while transcending the merely informative, is yet one of bringing about 'initiation into understanding the meaning of, and into questions about the truth and worth of, religion' (Smart, 1968, p. 105).

The RE teacher, like other teachers, might find it worthwhile to consider that the process of education, for the pupil, is not one which seeks to involve pupils in immediate engagement, but a process of learning what the world is like. Education is essentially a *study* of experience rather than the experience itself. It is no longer commonly thought that a pupil learns arithmetic in order to make sure he gets the right change at the local grocer's. Mathematics is now taught in order to bring the pupil to an understanding of mathematics. The aim of the history teacher is to get pupils to understand history rather than to 'engage' in history (whatever that might mean). Similar comments may be made of all curriculum areas. It might be expressed like this: if the world of experience – engineering, teaching, bus-driving, computer operating, and so on – is a world of 'first order' experience, then the process of education, a *study* of man's experience, is a 'second order' process. Seen in this way we can say that education is a process of bringing young people to the *threshold* of first order experience.

This is not to deny, of course, that there can be 'learning by doing'. What is sometimes forgotten is that 'learning' is the operative word, for that is the teacher's objective. The slogan can be taken to mean what it says, namely, that practical activities are often an efficient means of bringing about *learning*. What teachers cannot assume is that 'doing' and its equivalents are always a central part of method in education. It is often the case that education positively cannot (and sometimes should not) provide 'experience' within the field being studied. How would a West European schoolboy who never travels have 'practical experience' of a bushman, a cyclone, or Socrates? How would a pupil learn about sex, sin, or suttee? What matters within the context of slogans like 'learning by doing', 'learning by experience', and so on, is that the teacher shall recognize that *simulated* first order activities are often useful devices. The teacher of literature organizes a play for the school; the chemistry teacher gets pupils to prepare a foot powder for physical education lessons; the geography or history teacher arranges for pupils to visit an archaeological 'dig', and so on. But acting, and foot powder-making, and cleaning pottery shards are not in themselves the *objectives* of the educational process, or aspects of it; they are simulated 'real-life' situations contrived in order to produce in pupils a better understanding of literature, chemistry and history. There is a real distinction between working out a sum in order to get the correct answer and working out a sum in order to know what it means to work out sums.

Since there seems no good reason why RE, in a multi-cultural secular society, *should* have an educational goal different from other curriculum subjects, talk of engagement, commitment, or involvement in first order experience (whether purely religious, social, or moral) is bound to be looked upon with suspicion by the secular majority. Hence the continuing tension between those who wish to see RE on the timetable and those who do not, or who at most consider it best reduced to 'moral instruction' or some other non-religious subject. RE, therefore, may be seen, like 'education' as a whole, as a second order process with the aim of bringing pupils to a knowledge and understanding of religion. Any 'practical' activities involved (visiting places of worship, appreciating certain religious meanings by listening to Handel's *Messiah*, etc.) may be welcomed as a means to that end. But any practical activities posited as the 'end' or 'objective' of RE (e.g. to be religious, moral, co-operative in society, spiritual, etc.) can only be described as non-educational in so far as such activities would take the pupil *beyond* the threshold of education and into various forms of first order experience which belong, properly, to the educated individual rather than to the pupil in school.

In the light of these remarks the practice of corporate worship in schools is obviously not part of an educational process, strictly speaking. 'Worship' is a first order experience of the believer. No one, surely even the humanist or agnostic, would deny the beauty, the solemnity, the sheer religiousness of a well-organized junior school morning assembly praising God with 'Morning has broken'. But is it really necessary to maintain into the final decade of the twentieth century the argument that school worship is part of an educational process, the function of which is to study, not to practise, first order experience? In the final chapter of his book *School Worship: An Obituary*, John Hull makes suggestions for a reconstituted school assembly that would be 'free to serve the whole curriculum' (Hull, 1975, p. 122). It should not be necessary to say that such an assembly could not and should not be the preserve of the teacher of religion. Any attempt to place school assembly under the aegis of the RE teacher (which Hull's suggested programme would probably lead to, e.g. Hull's fourth objective includes the provision of 'some experience and understanding of what worship is') is likely to lead to forms of socializing or moralizing of pupils in one way rather than another and to raise RE in more subtle ways to a dominant position on the curriculum – a danger that Hull recognizes (p. 136) but does not escape.

Viewed as simply one more area of human experience to be *studied* (a second order activity) and in no way *practised* (a first order activity) – a confusion of the terms 'religion' and 'education' – RE should no longer have to defend itself against secular attacks for it is itself a 'secular' subject. One way of avoiding unnecessary criticism has been by means of a name change; another has been to suggest that we should only teach 'about' religion. On the question of name changes (Cox raises the question again in his *Problems and Possibilities for Religious Education*, 1983, p. 143), it would seem that, if the characterization of RE outlined above is essentially correct, the word 'religion' is all that is required of a subject title deemed to be parallel with 'English', 'mathematics', 'history' and 'science'; for 'education' is the name of the game and not an attribute of religion alone.

Teaching 'about' religion is, arguably, a verbal device aimed at preventing teachers from encouraging pupils to be religious in a first order sense. The phrase 'teaching about religion' is vague to the point of being meaningless since it can be qualified in a variety of ways to describe different forms of RE. For example, it can mean that we teach certain aspects of history, psychology, or sociology of religion, and this has been interpreted to mean that it is not *religion* that is being taught. Or we may teach 'about' religion with a very ordinary meaning of the word in mind, as when it is said 'I taught about cocoa production today', and clearly this does not preclude the teaching of religion in ways we have always taught it, with or without evangelistic aims. Consider Hirst's view (1974a, pp. 187–8):

> maintained schools should teach 'about' religion, provided that is interpreted to include a direct study of religions, which means entering as fully as possible into an understanding of what they claim to be true [which] will demand a great deal of imaginative involvement in expressions of religious life and even a form of engagement in these activities themselves. This must not, however, be confused with asking pupils to engage directly in any religious activities for the sake of these activities themselves.

Here, Hirst's qualifications of the word 'about' are quite specific in terms of what may and what may not be taught in RE and make the word 'about' unnecessary. Clearly nothing of substance needs to be seriously changed in the teaching of religion by use of the word 'about'. The indications are that there can be no better label for the material that ought to be taught in schools than 'religion'.

On a number of occasions I have hinted at the secular nature of religion as a curriculum subject in state schools. It could be argued that 'secular religion' is a contradiction in terms, for 'religion' seems by definition not to be secular. But for present purposes the phrase may be used to describe the formal teaching of religion – including claims to religious truth – within a secular society. Why should such a seemingly paradoxical expression be coined? It is intended to indicate that RE can be meaningfully taught in a way that would help to prevent on the one hand both overt and covert forms of 'confessionalism' and, on the other hand, would help to avoid a superficiality that can arise from teaching merely 'about' religion and from suggestions that we ought not to go into depth in the teaching of, for example, religious doctrines. The nature of education itself as a 'second order' process, briefly discussed on pages 82–3 (cf. also Sealey, 1979a) provides something of a framework for this approach.

Finally, it is suggested that a good reason why the RE teacher should adopt a philosophical approach to his work is that, in any search for meaning and clarity in the various positions taken up, progress in our understanding of the subject can only be made by constant critical appraisal of RE. Talk of 'critical appraisal' may remind religious believers of St John's injunction to 'try the spirits whether they are of God', a strictly religious or theological undertaking. As *teachers*, however, it is more appropriate for us to apply the secular rule of criticism proposed by Karl Popper, namely, that we attempt to refute the theory of our subject by solely rational means if we are to make progress in our understanding of the matters involved.

Summary of Chapter 6

In this chapter we have argued that the ever-expanding subject matter proposed for RE is not always appropriate and that theorists are mistaken if they see RE as the curriculum subject *par excellence*, alone or mainly able to deal with both global problems and the pupil's personal 'identity'.

We have argued that education is characteristically a study of, not an engagement in, human experience. Like other forms of 'first order' experience, therefore, school worship (for example) cannot be considered part of RE. And the idea of teaching 'about' religion is not a substitute for teaching religion in the depth it deserves nor a defence against evangelistic-type teaching.

Finally, it is suggested that RE should be regarded as yet one more secular subject, despite the apparent paradox this may imply. If this means a paradigm shift in our thinking then this can only be beneficial to an educational theory whose means of progress lies in our secular rational attempts to refute it.

*   *   *

7

Suggestions for Further Reading

Although there exists a vast literature on RE as a curriculum subject, comparatively few publications are especially concerned with the philosophical aspects of RE. We have, in the previous chapters, already met with much of this literature and, with one or two exceptions, I have not thought it necessary to comment on it again here. Readers who wish to pursue in more depth the issues discussed earlier are recommended to follow up that literature and the supporting references provided in it.

There is, of course, an enormous literature underpinning the philosophical aspects of religious education, particularly in the fields of philosophy of religion and philosophy of education. It is from this material that I have selected the following texts.

Discussion on the nature of religion and the claims made for the truth value of its statements is one of the biggest areas for study in the philosophy of religion. J. Hick's *Philosophy of Religion* (1963) introduces a range of important topics related to philosophical thinking about religion. His *The Existence of God* (1964) collects together more difficult but relevant arguments focused on theism. D. Z. Phillips's *Faith and Philosophical Enquiry* (1970) is well worth reading. Consisting of papers previously published in journals, it provides, from a Wittgenstein point of view, strong opposition to a strictly empirical approach to religious knowledge. It includes a chapter on religious education in which the views of P. H. Hirst (Hirst, 1965) are vigorously criticized. *Talk of God* (1969) (Royal Institute of Philosophy Lectures, Volume 2, 1967–8) contains essays on theism that would repay the reader searching for meaning within concepts central to theistic religion. William James's classic *The Varieties of Religious Experience* (1902), particularly Lecture 2, presents some guidance on the distinctiveness of religious experience. T. Penelhum has written a very readable and comprehensive introduction to philosophical thinking about religion in his *Religion and Rationality* (1971a), while his *Problems of Religious Knowledge* (1971b) focuses on the problematic nature of religious knowledge. A more traditional approach to problems in religious knowledge is provided by Hume's [1779] *Dialogues Concerning Natural Religion* and from a quite opposite point of view there is Kierkegaard's [1884] *Philosophical Fragments*. The status we give to RE in the school curriculum often depends on how we see religion and its place in the hierarchy of knowledge or the standing we are willing to give to religion within society. If religion is seen as one of Hirst's six or seven 'forms of knowledge' within his idea of a liberal education, then religion will be included for logical reasons. The same may be said of religion in the context of P. H. Phenix's *Realms of Meaning* (1964), for religion is there included within one of the six 'realms' deemed necessary for a 'general' education. Hirst criticizes Phenix's thesis in *Knowledge and the Curriculum* (1974a, ch. 4). Other perspectives on the justification of teaching religion are examined by J. White in his *Towards a Compulsory Curriculum* (1973), and by A. O'Hear in his *Education, Society and Human Nature* (1981). O'Hear (in ch. 4) also criticizes Hirst's 'forms of knowledge' thesis.

Smart's *Secular Education and the Logic of Religion* (1968) provides valuable insights into RE from a very general phenomenological point of view. His *The Phenomenon of Religion* (1973) goes into further explanatory detail. E. Sharpe has produced useful summaries of the method of phenomenology in his article 'The phenomenology of religion' (1975a) and in his *Comparative Religion: A History* (1975b).

The idea that teachers should teach 'about' religion still shows signs of life. R. F. Dearden, in his *The Philosophy of Primary Education* (1968), as well as P. H. Hirst in his paper 'Morals, religion and the maintained school' (reprinted in Hirst 1974a) and Barrow (1981) advocate this position. A number of useful essays are to be found in Sizer's *Religion and Public Education*, especially Part One (1967). R. Marples examines some of the relevant issues in his paper 'Is religious education possible?' (Marples, 1978). A reply to Marples by D. Attfield is to be found in the same volume (Attfield, 1978). My own article 'Teaching "about" and teaching "what is" in religion' (Sealey, 1979b) adds to the discussion.

A symposium led by C. Bailey and J. Elliott offers philosophical background for RE teachers on the concept of neutrality, a subject closely related to the idea of commitment (Bailey, 1973, and J. Elliott, 1973). Further discussion on the concept of indoctrination is to be found in *An Introduction to Philosophy of Education* (Woods and Barrow, 1975).

The relationship between ethics and religion is becoming an increasingly important area for debate. This is especially so among educationists concerned with RE. D. Little and B. Twiss, Jr, in their paper 'Basic terms in the study of religious ethics' (Outka and Reeder, 1973) show the complications involved in any attempt to disentangle the notions of religion as a guide to action and of morals as a guide to action. The collection of papers edited by P. Helm in *Divine Commands* and Morality (1981) covers many of the problem areas. R. B. Braithwaite's 'An empiricist's view of the nature of religious belief' attempts to reduce religious belief to a form of ethics. It is reproduced in Hick (1964) and Mitchell (1971). T. McPherson's *Philosophy and Religious Belief*, ch. 4, criticizes Braithwaite's theory (McPherson, 1974). H. J. Paton's *The Moral Law* (1948), a translation with commentary of Kant's *Groundwork of the Metaphysic of Morals*, is a valuable introduction to classical work on ethics that can also cast light on our understanding of the concept of a 'moral' God. Macy's *Let's Teach Them Right* (1969) brings together a number of contributions of varying philosophical interest on the problem of religious and moral education. Langford and O'Connor's *New Essays in the Philosophy of Education* (1973) includes a number of provocative papers of interest to RE teachers who wish to consider further the philosophical aspects of moral and religious education within the context of the philosophy of education.

References

Acland, R. (1964), *We Teach Them Wrong* (London: Gollancz).

Aga Khan and Zaki Ali (1944), *Glimpses of Islam* (Lahore: Ashraf Publications).

Alves, C. (1972), *The Christian in Education* (London: SCM Press).

Alves, C. (1975), 'Why religious education?', in Smart and Horder, 1975, p. 26.

Atkinson, R. F. (1965), 'Instruction and indoctrination', in R. D. Archambault (ed.), *Philosophical Analysis and Education* (London: Routledge & Kegan Paul), p. 173.

Attfield, D. (1978), 'Is religious education possible? A reply to Roger Marples', *Journal of Philosophy of Education*, vol. 12, pp. 93–7.

Audah, Abdul Q. (1971), *Between Ignorant Followers and Incapable Scholars*, International Islamic Federation of Student Organizations, No. 6 (Salmijah: Kuwait).

Ayer, A. J. [1936], *Language, Truth and Logic* (London: Gollancz, 1946).

Baier, K. (1973), 'Moral autonomy as an aim of moral education', in Langford and O'Connor, 1973, p. 108.

Bailey, C. (1973), 'Teaching by discussion and the neutral teacher', *Proceedings of the Philosophy of Education Society of Great Britain*, vol. 7, no. 1, pp. 26–38.

Barrow, R. (1981), *The Philosophy of Schooling* (Brighton: Harvester).

Bhagavad Gita, Juan Mascaró translation (Harmondsworth: Penguin, 1962).

Birmingham (1975a), *Agreed Syllabus of Religious Instruction* (Birmingham: City of Birmingham Education Committee).

Birmingham (1975b), *Living Together: A Teacher's Handbook of Suggestions for Religious Education* (Birmingham: City of Birmingham Education Committee).

Brent, A. (1978), *Philosophical Foundations for the Curriculum* (London: Allen & Unwin).

Cambridge (1949), *Cambridgeshire Agreed Syllabus* (Cambridge: Cambridgeshire Education Authority).

Casey, J. (1973), 'The anatomy of art', in *Philosophy and the Arts*, Royal Institute of Philosophy Lectures, Vol. 6, 1971–2 (London: Macmillan), p. 80.

Cox, E. (1966), *Changing Aims in Religious Education* (London: Routledge & Kegan Paul).

Cox, E. (1976), 'Does it do as it says?', *Learning for Living*, vol. 15, no. 4, p. 126.

Cox, E. (1983), *Problems and Possibilities for Religious Education* (Sevenoaks: Hodder & Stoughton).

Dearden, R. F. (1968), *The Philosophy of Primary Education* (London: Routledge & Kegan Paul).

Dorset (1979), *Agreed Syllabus of Religious Education* (Dorchester: Dorset County Council).

Droubie, Riadhe el (1978), 'Religious education: a Muslim insight', in W. Owen Cole (ed.), *World Faiths in Education* (London: Allen & Unwin), pp. 161–2.

90

REFERENCES

Dudley (1979), *Agreed Syllabus of Religious Education* (Dudley: Dudley Metropolitan Borough Education Services).

Elliott, J. (1973), 'Neutrality, rationality and the role of the teacher', *Proceedings of the Philosophy of Education Society of Great Britain*, vol. 7, no. 1, pp. 39–65.

Elliott, R. K. (1973), 'Imagination in the experience of art', in *Philosophy and the Arts*, Royal Institute of Philosophy Lectures, Vol. 6, 1971–2 (London: Macmillan), pp. 102–3.

Flew, A. G. N. (1972), 'Indoctrination and religion', in I. A. Snook (ed.), *Concepts of Indoctrination* (London: Routledge & Kegan Paul), pp. 75, 106.

Flew, A. G. N., and MacIntyre, A. (eds) (1955), *New Essays in Philosophical Theology* (London: SCM Press).

Gardner, P. (1980), 'Religious education: in defence of non-commitment', *Journal of Philosophy of Education*, vol. 14, no. 2, p. 163.

Gedge, P. (1975), 'Morals and religion', in Smart and Horder, 1975, p. 51.

Goldman, R. (1964), *Religious Thinking from Childhood to Adolescence* (London: Routledge & Kegan Paul).

Goldman, R. (1965), *Readiness for Religion* (London: Routledge & Kegan Paul).

Gribble, J. (1969), *Introduction to Philosophy of Education* (Boston, Mass.: Allyn & Bacon).

Grimmitt, M. (1973), *What Can I Do In RE?* (Great Wakering: Mayhew-McCrimmon).

Grimmitt, M. (1981), 'When is "commitment" a problem in religious education?', *British Journal of Educational Studies*, vol. 29, no. 1, pp. 43, 46, 48–9, 51.

Grimmitt, M. (1982), 'World religions and personal development', in R. Jackson (ed.), *Approaching World Religions* (London: John Murray), pp. 141, 143.

Hamlyn, D. W. (1972), 'Objectivity', in R. F. Dearden, P. H. Hirst and R. S. Peters (eds), *Education and the Development of Reason*, Pt 2 (London: Routledge & Kegan Paul), p. 107.

Hampshire (1978), *Religious Education in Hampshire Schools* (Hampshire: Hampshire Education Authority).

Hardy, D. W. (1979), 'Truth in religious education: further reflections on the implications of pluralism', *British Journal of Religious Education*, vol. 1, no. 3, p. 107.

Hare, R. M. (1955), 'Theology and falsification', in Flew and MacIntyre, 1955, ch. VI, s. B, p. 101.

Harris, A. (1970), *Thinking About Education* (London: Heinemann).

Helm, P. (ed.) (1981), *Divine Commands and Morality* (Oxford: OUP).

Hick, J. (1963), *Philosophy of Religion* (Englewood Cliffs, NJ: Prentice-Hall).

Hick, J. (1964) (ed.), *The Existence of God* (New York: Macmillan).

Hirst, P. H. (1965), 'Morals, religion and the maintained school', *British Journal of Educational Studies*, vol. 14, no. 1, pp. 5–18.

Hirst, P. H. (1974a), *Knowledge and the Curriculum* (London: Routledge & Kegan Paul).

Hirst, P. H. (1974b), *Moral Education in a Secular Society* (London: University of London Press).

Hirst, P. H., and Peters, R. S. (1970), *Logic of Education* (London: Routledge & Kegan Paul).

Holley, R. (1978), *Religious Education and Religious Understanding* (London: Routledge & Kegan Paul).

Hudson, W. D. (1973), 'Is religious education possible?', in Langford and O'Connor, 1973, p. 190.

Hudson, W. D. (1974), *A Philosophical Approach to Religion* (London: Macmillan).

Hull, J. M. (1975), *School Worship: An Obituary* (London: SCM Press).

Hull, J. M. (1976), 'Religious indoctrination in the Birmingham Agreed Syllabus?', *Faith and Freedom*, vol. 30, no. 88, pp. 30, 32–3, 35.

Hulmes, E. (1979), *Commitment and Neutrality in Religious Education* (London: Geoffrey Chapman).

Hume, D. [1779], *Dialogues Concerning Natural Religion* (New York: Hafner Press, 1948).

James, W. (1902), *The Varieties of Religious Experience* (New York: Longmans, Green).

Kierkegaard, S. [1844], *Philosophical Fragments* (Princeton, NJ: Princeton University Press, 1962).

Kolakowski, L. (1978), *Main Currents of Marxism* (Oxford: Clarendon Press).

Langford, G., and O'Connor, D. J. (eds) (1973), *New Essays in the Philosophy of Education* (London: Routledge & Kegan Paul).

Loukes, H. (1961), *Teenage Religion* (London: SCM Press).

Loukes, H. (1965), *New Ground in Christian Education* (London: SCM Press).

Macy, C. (ed.) (1969), *Let's Teach Them Right* (London: Pemberton Books).

Malcolm, N. (1967), 'Knowledge and belief', in A. Phillips Griffiths (ed.), *Knowledge and Belief* (London: OUP), pp. 72–3.

Marples, R. (1978), 'Is religious education possible?', in *Journal of Philosophy of Education*, vol. 12, pp. 81–91.

McPherson, T. (1974), *Philosophy and Religious Belief* (London: Hutchinson).

Mitchell, B. (ed.) (1971), *The Philosophy of Religion* (London: OUP).

Newsom, J. (1963), *Half Our Future: Report of the Central Advisory Council for Education (England)* (London: HMSO).

Oakeshott, M. (1933), *Experience and its Modes* (Cambridge: CUP).

O'Hear, A. (1981), *Education, Society and Human Nature* (London: Routledge & Kegan Paul).

Outka, G., and Reeder, J. P. (eds) (1973), *Religion and Morality* (New York: Anchor Books).

Paton, H. J. (1948), *The Moral Law* (London: Hutchinson).

Penelhum, T. (1971a) *Religion and Rationality* (New York: Random House).

Penelhum, T. (1971b), *Problems of Religious Knowledge* (New York: Random House).

Peters, R. S. (1964), *Education as Initiation* (London: Harrap).

Phenix, P. H. (1964), *Realms of Meaning* (New York: McGraw-Hill).

Phillips, D. Z. (1965), *The Concept of Prayer* (London: Routledge & Kegan Paul).

Phillips, D. Z. (1970), *Faith and Philosophical Enquiry* (London: Routledge & Kegan Paul).

Plowden, B. (1967), *Children and Their Primary Schools: A Report of the Central Advisory Council for Education (England)*, Vol. 1 (London: HMSO).

Pring, R. (1972) 'Knowledge out of control', *Education for Teaching*, no. 89 (Autumn), p. 25.

Schools Council (1971), Working Paper 36, *Religious Education in Secondary Schools* (London: Evans/Methuen).

Sealey, J. A. (1970), *Know Your Town: Sketches in Local History* (Rugby: Local History Publications).

Sealey, J. A. (1979a), 'Education as a second order form of experience and its relation to religion', *Journal of Philosophy of Education*, vol. 13, pp. 83–90.

Sealey, J. A. (1979b), 'Teaching "about" and teaching "what is" in religion', *British Journal of Religious Education*, vol. 2, no. 2, pp. 56–60.

Sen, K. M. (1961), *Hinduism* (Harmondsworth: Penguin).

Sharpe, E. J. (1975a), 'The phenomenology of religion', *Learning for Living*, vol. 15, no. 1, pp. 4–9.

Sharpe, E. J. (1975b), *Comparative Religion: A History* (London: Duckworth).

Sizer, T. R. (ed.) (1967), *Religion and Public Education* (Boston, Mass.: Houghton Mifflin).

Smart, N. (1968), *Secular Education and the Logic of Religion* (London: Faber).

Smart, N. (1969), 'The comparative study of religion in schools', in Macy, 1969, pp. 63–5.

Smart, N. (1970), *The Philosophy of Religion* (New York: Random House).

Smart, N. (1973), *The Phenomenon of Religion* (London: Macmillan).

Smart, N., and Horder, D. (eds) (1975), *New Movements in Religious Education* (London: Temple Smith).

Smith, J. W. D. (1975), *Religion and Secular Education* (Edinburgh: St Andrew Press).

Talk of God (1969), Royal Institute of Philosophy Lectures, Vol. 2, 1967–8 (London: Macmillan).

Trigg, R. (1973), *Reason and Commitment* (Cambridge: CUP).

West Riding (1966), *West Riding Agreed Syllabus (Suggestions for Religious Education)* (Wakefield: County Education Offices).

White, J. (1967), 'Indoctrination', in R. S. Peters (ed.), *The Concept of Education* (London: Routledge & Kegan Paul), pp. 181, 189, 190.

White, J. (1973), *Towards a Compulsory Curriculum* (London: Routledge & Kegan Paul).

Wilson, J. (1964), 'Education and indoctrination', in T. H. B. Hollins (ed.), *Aims in Education* (Manchester: Manchester University Press), pp. 26, 28, 34.

Wilson, J. (1971), *Education in Religion and the Emotions* (London: Heinemann).

Wilson, J. (1976), 'Taking religious education seriously', *Learning for Living*, vol. 16, no. 1, pp. 21–3.

Wilson, J., Williams, N., and Sugarman, B. (1967), *Introduction to Moral Education* (Harmondsworth: Penguin).

Winch, P. (1958), *The Idea of a Social Science and its Relation to Philosophy* (London: Routledge & Kegan Paul).

Wisdom, J. (1953), 'Gods', in his *Philosophy and Psychoanalysis* (Oxford: Blackwell), p. 158.

Wittgenstein, L. (1958), *Philosophical Investigations* (Oxford: Blackwell).

Wittgenstein, L. (1969), *On Certainty* (Oxford: Blackwell).

Woods, R. G., and Barrow, R. St C. (1975), *An Introduction to Philosophy of Education* (London: Methuen).

Index

95